Social Scie~~n~~
Beyond th~~e Academy~~

Social Science Careers Beyond the Academy provides a "road-map" to a career outside of academia for students of the social sciences who want to transition to a corporate or government environment after they complete their studies.

It isn't always easy to see how the skills you develop in academia will apply to corporate consultancy or research positions, or even to see clearly where these various career paths might lead and whether they might suit you. Are you a start-up person or do you think that a big, established organization will provide you with desirable opportunities? Would you prefer to work for a public or private firm, or perhaps for a government agency? Are you better at research or project management? How do you go about adapting your writing to the non-specialist audience of colleagues in an organization?

This book is written by a team of authors who straddle the line that separates academia from consultancy work and have mentored countless students to make a successful transition to the working world, whether in academia or not. The authors identify and categorize various popular paths that are available to you; describe the types of organization, roles, and what they involve; and show how to map your own skills, personality, and preferences to the jobs you might aspire to obtain. This book is the ultimate guide to building your path to success after you conclude your studies.

Using an informal style, this book is ideal for social science students looking to make their next steps after academia by seeking positions in consulting and research firms, or with a government entity.

Stacey S. Merola, Ph.D., is a Principal Investigator at Guidehouse, Inc. where she is providing leadership on a portfolio of large, mixed-methods evaluations. Dr. Merola is a multiple award-winning evaluator with more than 25 years of social science research experience and over 20 years of experience in program evaluation, as both a manager and an analyst. Over the course of her career, Dr. Merola has worked with a diverse cross section of clientele representing government, corporations, and nonprofits to understand the effectiveness of their programs. She has worked at large consulting firms and small consulting firms, and owned her own successful small business for eight years.

John Hitchcock, Ph.D. (University at Albany, State University of New York), is a Principal Research Scientist at Westat, where he conducts grant-funded and contract-based research for government agencies and philanthropies. He focuses on evaluating interventions in K–12 education and he writes about mixed methods research and other types of research designs. To date he co-authored more than 70 works that have been collectively cited more than 6,000 times and he presented at professional conferences more than 150 times. He worked as a tenured faculty member at two different universities.

Mercedes Rubio, Ph.D., is Program Director in the Division of Training, Workforce Development, and Diversity, where she handles the National Research Mentoring Network (NRMN) of the NIH Common Fund Enhancing the Diversity of the NIH-funded Workforce Initiative, the Institutional Research and Academic Career Development Awards (IRACDA), the Bridges to the Baccalaureate, Innovative Programs to Enhance Research Training (IPERT), and the Research to Understand and Inform Interventions that Promote the Research Careers of Students in Biomedical and Behavioral Sciences portfolios. She also will serve in the role of program officer in the NIGMS Postdoctoral Research Associate (PRAT) Program. Before joining NIGMS, Rubio was chief of the Psychopathology Risk and Protective Factors Research Program at the National Institute of Mental Health and was assistant director of that Institute's Individual Research Fellowship Program. Rubio earned a B.A. in sociology from California State University, Bakersfield, and a Ph.D. in medical sociology from the University of Michigan, Ann Arbor, where she also completed postdoctoral training in nursing in the area of HIV intervention and health disparities.

STACEY S. MEROLA,
JOHN HITCHCOCK, AND
MERCEDES RUBIO

Social Science Careers

Beyond the Academy

Finding a Path in Consulting and Government Settings

LONDON AND NEW YORK

Designed cover image: © Getty Images

First published 2023
by Routledge
4 Park Square, Milton Park, Abingdon, Oxon OX14 4RN

and by Routledge
605 Third Avenue, New York, NY 10158

Routledge is an imprint of the Taylor & Francis Group, an informa business

British Library Cataloguing-in-Publication Data
A catalogue record for this book is available from the British Library

Library of Congress Cataloging-in-Publication Data
Names: Merola, Stacey S., author. | Hitchcock, John H. (Educational psychologist), author. | Rubio, Mercedes (Program director), author.
Title: Outside the academy: discover social science careers in consulting and government settings: your guide to choosing the career path that will make the best use of your skills/Stacey S. Merola, John Hitchcock, Mercedes Rubio.
Description: Abingdon, Oxon; New York, NY: Routledge, 2023. | Includes bibliographical references and index.
Identifiers: LCCN 2022039578 (print) | LCCN 2022039579 (ebook) | ISBN 9780367356347 (hardback) | ISBN 9781032432861 (paperback) | ISBN 9780367815974 (ebook)
Subjects: LCSH: Social sciences—Vocational guidance. | Social scientists. | Civil service. | Consultants.
Classification: LCC H61 .M49125 2023 (print) | LCC H61 (ebook) | DDC 300.2—dc23/eng/20220907
LC record available at https://lccn.loc.gov/2022039578
LC ebook record available at https://lccn.loc.gov/2022039579

ISBN: 978-0-367-35634-7 (hbk)
ISBN: 978-1-032-43286-1 (pbk)
ISBN: 978-0-367-81597-4 (ebk)

DOI: 10.4324/9780367815974

Typeset in Joanna MT
by Apex CoVantage, LLC

Contents

List of Figures and Tables   vii
Acknowledgments   viii

Can I Pick Your Brain? One   1
The Ideal Versus the Reality of Academic Careers   1.1   3
Graduation and Employment Trends in the
Social Sciences   1.2   5
Given These Questions, We Turn to the Goal
of This Book   1.3   8
Getting the Lay of the Land – How to Read This Book
and Introducing Its Three Authors   1.4   10

What Types of Organizations Would Hire Me? Two   14
Government Agencies   2.1   14
Government Contractors   2.2   14
Think Tanks   2.3   15
Consulting Firms   2.4   16
General Private Industry   2.5   16
Nonprofit and Philanthropic Organizations   2.6   17

**What Types of Jobs Would I Be Hired for and
What Are the Typical Tasks? Three   20**
Types of Jobs   3.1   20
Program Evaluation   3.1.1   22
Typical Tasks   3.2   23
Government Agencies   3.3   25
Consulting Firms   3.4   25
Project Management   3.4.1   28
Think Tanks   3.5   29
Private Industry, Nonprofit Organizations,
and Philanthropies   3.6   29

What Skills Will I Need? **Four** 31
Historically Important Social Science Skills 4.1 33
Important Skills in the Near Term (Potentially) 4.2 39
Job Skills and Research Methods 4.3 40

How Do I Get These Jobs? **Five** 49
Interviews 5.1 52

What If I Want to Work for the Government? **Six** 57
Tips for Getting Started 6.1 59
Tips for Making It Through the Certification Process 6.2 59
Resume/Curriculum Vitae (CV) 6.2.1 59
GS Pay Scale 6.2.2 61
Informational Interviews 6.2.3 62
Reading Job Announcement Postings 6.2.4 64
Assessment Questions 6.2.5 68
Human Resources 6.2.6 71
Decision Points After the Certification Process 6.3 72
First Decision Point: Candidate's Resumes/CVs Are Reviewed 6.3.1 72
Second Decision Point: Interview Process 6.3.2 72
Third Decision Point: Selection Process 6.3.3 74
Job Offer and Onboarding 6.3.4 75
Alternative Routes to Entering the Federal Government 6.4 76

What If I Decide I Want to Go (Back)
Into Academics? **Seven** 78
"Jonah's" Career Path Story 7.1 80

What If I Want to Have My Own Business? **Eight** 89
What Services Are You Going to Provide? 8.1 91
Who Will Be Your Clients? 8.2 92
How Will You Market Yourself? 8.3 92
How Should I Structure My Business? 8.4 94
What Are the Interim and End Goals? 8.5 96

What If I Can't Decide and Want to Do Both? **Nine** 98
Any More Advice on How to Get There? 9.1 102

Can You Give Me Any Other Help With
My Existential Angst? **Ten** 103

Index 105

FIGURES

1.1	Twenty-year Historical Trends in Post-graduation Employment Sector Commitments of Psychologists and Other Social Scientists, 1999–2019	8
6.1	Position Open & Closing Dates and Pay Scale and Grade	64
6.2	Example of Job Posting Open to Non-Federal Employees	65
6.3	Example of Job Posting Open to Federal Employees	65
6.4	Example of Duties in Federal Job Posting	66
6.5	Information About Candidate Qualifications	67
6.6	Educational Attainment as a Way to Qualify for a Job Announcement	68
6.7	"How to Apply" Guidance	69
7.1	The Rare Times One Finds Research One Really Wants to Do and Is Paid to Do It	84
10.1	Non-academic Careers Decision Tree	104

TABLES

1.1	Changes in the Numbers of Ph.D. Recipients by Social Science Discipline Between 1990 and 2020	5
1.2	Post-graduation Employment Plans of Doctoral Recipients in the Social Sciences, 2020	7
1.3	Book Chapters Overview	11
1.4	Author Bios	11
2.1	Organization Type and Characteristics That Typically Hire Social Scientists	15
4.1	Contemporary Research Methods Needs	41

We would like to thank all the graduate students and professionals who trusted us with their questions over the years. We hope our answers have been helpful to you.

We would like to thank the publishers at Routledge for their patience, flexibility, and support throughout the writing process. We would also like to thank our family and friends for not asking too many times when this book was finally going to be completed.

Stacey would like to thank Noelle Chesley for encouraging her years ago to write about her life. She would also like to thank Patrick Merla and Amy Schoen for their advice and suggestions during the various stages of writing this book.

One

"Hey! I just formed an LLC[1] so I can go after my own consulting work. Would you be up for drinks or coffee in the next few weeks so I can pick your brain?" A friend was embarking on a journey that Stacey, one of the coauthors of this book, had started on almost exactly eight years before and wanted advice. Stacey received many requests to talk about having a business, changing careers, becoming an evaluator, or going into non-academic careers with many people before, so she was happy to oblige. This book was inspired by these requests and their underlying premise that information regarding careers outside of academics is not easily available to social scientists and that there is insufficient discussion of these options in most graduate programs. These questions, relevant prior to the coronavirus pandemic due to the small ratio of tenure-track jobs to Ph.D. graduates, have become even more salient in the aftermath of a pandemic that caused an overall reduction in the higher education workforce of 13%.[2]

The pandemic has changed the way we work around the world. People, particularly knowledge workers, increasingly work from home across multiple sectors of the economy and meetings take place virtually. Likewise, academic conferences and instruction have gone increasingly virtual. Though originally viewed as a temporary measure, some institutions are making remote work permanent with the implications for hiring, career trajectories, and salaries still to be determined.[3] This turn of events could open up jobs to people unable to relocate due to family demands or other circumstances; however, salaries could also be depressed as institutions hire candidates in locations with lower costs of living. John, one of the book's coauthors, was able to take a new job precisely because of the increased reliance on a remote workforce. He had been interested in leaving a tenured job in academia because he knew he could get a job in research contracting performing the same work his university was asking him to do but receive a better salary and working conditions for his efforts. John made his move prior to the onset of the

DOI: 10.4324/9780367815974-1

pandemic because more and more companies had started to allow for remote work. But he was worried about being dependent on the only company that afforded the flexibility he preferred. Since the pandemic, we have noted that most companies are now acclimated to remote workers joining meetings through some Internet meeting platform or another. Hence, this is a game changer, and readers of this book will be interested in how to navigate this new flexibility. This is all covered later in the book but, at the outset, we argue that though there might be changes in "how" we work and "where" we work, the fundamentals of "what" we are working on and "why" we are doing the work has not changed. The world of remote work has changed so much that we think every graduate student in a social science program should read this book.

Indeed, in some ways it has never been a better time to be an applied social scientist because, sadly, we live in interesting times. Solutions to societal problems require research and evidence. Policymakers and the general public look for answers in challenging times. For example, data visualizations have become part of daily life during the pandemic (e.g., major newspapers in the United States routinely present such visualizations) and are likely here to stay. Philanthropies and nonprofits have moved toward models of program evaluation that promote equity, and there is greater recognition of so-called wicked problems (i.e., tough problems to solve). For example, during the 2020 demonstrations after the killing of George Floyd, former President Barack Obama held a town hall on evidence-based interventions to reduce police violence.[4] The Foundations for Evidence-Based Policymaking Act (Evidence Act) of 2019 changed how agencies make policy decisions, requiring agencies to create learning agendas and evaluation plans to foster data-driven decision-making.[5] With these trends and more, the research skills gained while obtaining a Ph.D. in one of the social science fields will have wide applicability. There is no shortage of other wicked problems; we social scientists have a role in understanding, predicting, and influencing human behavior around climate change, vaccine programming, income inequality, chronic health concerns and disparities in these concerns, information literacy (and illiteracy), violence, and to end on a more positive note, educating future generations to operate in a workforce that will see expansive changes in technology and cross-cultural interactions. We, the authors of this book, think we have some insights on the opportunities this all presents to social scientists who work outside of academia, and so this book was written for anyone who does not yet know a lot about social science careers outside of standard academia, in the United States, and might wish to "pick our brains" (this phrase yields some odd imagery, doesn't it?).

1.1 THE IDEAL VERSUS THE REALITY OF ACADEMIC CAREERS

The idealized academic career is one of clear milestones, which continues, in most cases, over 20 years of achievement. After completing one's dissertation, one obtains a tenure-track job as an assistant professor. As an assistant professor, the typical task at hand is to publish one's dissertation in a peer-reviewed journal and a number of other papers, all while teaching courses, and presenting at conferences. Maybe you will also publish a book. After about six years of hard work (on top of the 20–25 years of schooling), you earn the gold ring: tenure as an associate professor, with the near-promise of lifetime employment. After this you keep working toward becoming a full professor, possibly even an endowed chair, followed by semi-retirement as an emeritus professor, having left behind a record of published books, papers, etc., along the way.

Unfortunately, the gap between reality and the ideal has been growing over time. Tenure-track jobs do provide security and prestige, but they are becoming increasingly hard to get. Much has been written about the "adjunctification" of higher education. The American Association of University Professors (AAUP) found that in 2016, 73% of instructional positions at U.S. institutions of higher education were non-tenure track.[6] These non-tenure-track positions are often low paying (and in some cases non-paying as was evidenced in a 2022 controversy over a non-paying adjunct job at UCLA that required a Ph.D. in chemistry or biochemistry, a strong teaching record at the college level, and three to five letters of recommendation).[7] In a pre-pandemic, national survey of contingent faculty conducted in 2019 by the American Federation of Teachers, 25% reported relying on public assistance and 40%, almost half, had trouble meeting their basic household expenses.[8] Even if you do gain tenure, this does not prevent potential job losses due to whole departments being disbanded or other cutbacks related to external events. For example, shutdowns and instructional changes related to the COVID-19 pandemic have led to departmental restructuring. We even have relationships with former faculty who, sadly, lost their jobs despite being tenured, full professors with strong teaching and publication records. This remains a rare event, but it does happen, and further establishes our point that there seems to be a widening gap between the ideal academic career and reality.

It is also true that the traditional academic career path may not be desirable for all people. The demanding nature of academic jobs is well documented. In traditional sociological literature, academia may be described as a "greedy institution," where the assumption is that one is willing to sacrifice everything (i.e., family time, preferred location) for the job.[9] This is also a traditionally masculine path (and further a traditionally white, masculine path), with an underlying assumption that one has a spouse willing to follow where the academic career leads, and willing to take on the bulk of family responsibilities.[10] The hours are long, pay is relatively low, and professors may be challenged by pregnancies, sickness, etc., due to lack of traditional sick time. Academic jobs have traditionally been flexible (as we joked in graduate school, you can pick which 80 hours a week you want to work); however, with advances in technology over time, other jobs are becoming more flexible, allowing people to pick when and where they work.

As an aside, it occurs to us that some readers might be surprised by this "greedy institution" observation because the professoriate has at different turns been romanticized and criticized. There is plenty of media with imagery of bearded male professors in the United States who work 20 hours a week so that they can smoke a pipe while wearing a cardigan sweater, except when they wear white during the summer to write a book at a lake house (the female professor archetype is less palatable, and there is little media imagery of gender fluid academics as of this writing). Open your preferred search engine and search for the phrase "lazy professor," and you'll find no shortage of deconstructive criticism. There are whole books dedicated to critiquing and we daresay attacking the role. We normally would cite these works to further back our claim but, if this is not clear already, this book is not meant to be pitched as an academic work; we tried for a quick read because if you have a doctoral degree or are trying to earn one, then you do not need another scholarly tome that badly taxes your time and cognitive energy.[11] The truth is, academic positions come with a lot of work.[12] John was a professor for ten years and not once was he able to take a summer off; he might have worked a little less and his work was different during the summer, but work he did between June through August.

So, given the well-documented lack of jobs, and structural barriers for many groups, where are people working? Data on employment trends in the social sciences can provide some insights.

1.2 GRADUATION AND EMPLOYMENT TRENDS IN THE SOCIAL SCIENCES

So how many people are graduating with Ph.D.s in the social sciences in the United States? The National Science Foundation (NSF) has been collecting data on the numbers and demographic characteristics of people graduating with Ph.D.s since the 1950s. Looking at trends over the last 30 years, between 1990 and 2020 there was an overall increase in the numbers of people earning Ph.D.s in social science disciplines (Table 1.1). The total number of social science Ph.D. recipients increased from 14,199 in 1990 to 15,721 in 2020, a 10.7% increase. That figure masks the fact that some disciplines had increases in numbers over this time period while others had decreases. Overall, economics, business administration, and "other social sciences"[13] were the only disciplines to experience steady increases in the numbers of students achieving Ph.D.s over the 30 years between 1990 and 2020. Overall, there was a 122% increase in the numbers of Ph.D.s awarded between 1990 and 2020.

Table 1.1 Changes in the Numbers of Ph.D. Recipients by Social Science Discipline Between 1990 and 2020

Discipline	1990	2000	2010	2020	% Change 1990– 2000	% Change 2000– 2010	% Change 2010– 2020
Psychology	3,281	3,616	3,420	3,879	10%	−5%	13%
Anthropology	324	446	507	448	38%	14%	−17%
Economics	862	948	1,073	1,216	10%	13%	13%
Political science and government	462	669	728	637	45%	9%	−13%
Sociology	428	617	639	607	44%	4%	−5%
Other social sciences	974	1,156	1,515	2,159	19%	31%	43%
Education administration	1,664	2,036	1,439	927	22%	−29%	−36%
Education research	2,439	2,667	2,443	2,312	9%	−8%	−5%
Teacher education	419	261	245	113	−38%	−6%	−54%
Teaching fields	922	824	799	940	−11%	−3%	18%
Other education	1,065	654	361	424	−39%	−45%	17%
Business management and administration	1,036	1,065	1,366	1,466	3%	28%	7%
Communication	323	389	638	593	20%	64%	−7%
Total	14,199	15,348	15,173	15,721	8%	−1%	4%

Source: National Science Foundation, National Center for Science and Engineering Statistics, Survey of Earned Doctorates, 2020

Other social science fields experienced fluctuations in rates across these time periods. There were relatively large increases in the number of Ph.D.s in political science and government, sociology, anthropology, and education administration between 1990 and 2000, trends that were a continuation of the large growth in the numbers of Ph.D.s awarded beginning after the Second World War.[14] The communication field had its largest increases between the years 2000 and 2010. The numbers of Ph.D.s awarded in Psychology, Teaching fields, and "Other education" jumped between 2010 and 2020.

What trends have there been in where these doctoral recipients right after graduation? Based on the latest data available from 2020 (which coincided with the start of the COVID-19 pandemic), there were higher percentages of social science doctoral recipients reporting that they had no definite work commitments (Table 1.2.). The economic and social conditions resulting from the pandemic undoubtedly influenced some of these trends. It is hard to predict employment trends for new doctoral recipients after the pandemic, but we can look at historical trends up to 2019.

Prior to the pandemic in 2019, unemployment was at its lowest rate in 50 years at 3.5%.[15] Figure 1.1. depicts historical trends in the sectors where social science Ph.D.-recipients found employment after graduation. As of 2019, there had been a ten-year decline from 2009 in the percentage of Ph.D. recipients who were committed to work in academia after graduation. Concurrently there was a ten-year upward trend in Ph.D. recipients who were committed to work in the industry after graduation.

Given all of this rapid change and choices in the types of jobs that are available, it is not surprising that we, the three authors of this book, have received a lot of questions from graduate students, recently minted Ph.D.s,[16] and mid-career folks with doctoral degrees. Here is a sampling of these questions:

- How can I set myself up to get a job in academia?
- I'm thinking about leaving academia; how do you like the work you are doing now?
- Do you have any advice on getting a job with the federal government?
- What would be some good classes to take if I want a career in evaluation?
- What types of jobs are there in your industry?

Table 1.2 Post-graduation Employment Plans of Doctoral Recipients in the Social Sciences, 2020

Field of Study	All Recipients	Recipients With Definite Commitments	Recipients With no Definite Commitments	Postdoctoral Study in the United States	Academic Employment in the United States	Industry Employment in the United States[a]	Other Work in the United States[b]	Work Abroad
Psychology	3,879	68%	32%	40%	11%	8%	8%	2%
Anthropology	448	55%	45%	16%	19%	2%	9%	9%
Economics	1,216	76%	24%	11%	19%	16%	11%	19%
Political science and government	637	70%	30%	20%	27%	5%	8%	9%
Sociology	607	71%	29%	17%	35%	4%	7%	7%
Other social sciences	2,159	62%	38%	13%	22%	6%	13%	9%
Education administration	927	70%	30%	1%	27%	3%	36%	2%
Education research	2,312	67%	33%	8%	32%	5%	17%	4%
Teacher education	113	58%	42%	D	29%	D	18%	6%
Teaching fields	940	64%	36%	6%	32%	3%	17%	6%
Other education	424	60%	40%	D	25%	D	22%	4%
Business management and administration	1,466	72%	28%	3%	44%	8%	5%	11%
Communication	593	64%	36%	8%	40%	6%	4%	7%

D – Suppressed to avoid disclosure of confidential information

a: Includes doctorate recipients who indicated self-employment.

b: Includes doctorate recipients who indicated government, nonprofit, elementary or secondary school, or other employment and those with unknown employment.

Source: National Science Foundation, National Center for Science and Engineering Statistics, Survey of Earned Doctorates, 2020

7   **Can I Pick Your Brain?**

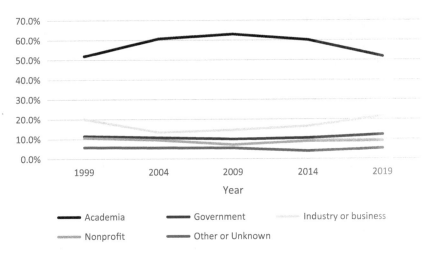

Figure 1.1 Twenty-year Historical Trends in Post-graduation Employment Sector Commitments of Psychologists and Other Social Scientists, 1999–2019

Note: Does not include Ph.D. recipients in education.
Source: National Science Foundation, National Center for Science and Engineering Statistics, Survey of Earned Doctorates, 2020

- What are the different kinds of firms in your industry?
- What advice can you give me about seeking grants?

And let's not forget the question presented at the opening of this chapter: Hey! I just formed an LLC so I can go after my own consulting work. Would you be up for drinks or coffee in the next few weeks so I can pick your brain?

1.3 GIVEN THESE QUESTIONS, WE TURN TO THE GOAL OF THIS BOOK

The goal of this book is not to rehash the pros and cons of becoming an academic but rather to provide general information about jobs outside of academia for post-graduate students in the social sciences, as well as others who might be considering a career change, whether that be between academic and non-academic careers or even between the non-academic sectors described here. Our focus is on careers in research consulting firms, government positions, and some insights about operating a small research consulting business because we, the authors, have collective experience with these types of jobs. Although we touch on social science careers working for organizations that have a mission other than research consulting (e.g., working as an industrial-organizational psychologist for a large manufacturer, as an economist for a major distributor), we do not describe such work in detail because it falls outside of our collective experience. Similarly, social scientists might have the training needed to pursue work in clinical/service settings (e.g., psychologists, social work), and we do not discuss these pathways in detail because, again, our related experience in these arenas is minimal. This book does offer some insights into ways to avoid treating pursuit of an academic career versus a non-academic career as a dichotomy. The traditional way to think about an academic career is described earlier, but it can be possible to pursue other combinations. One can be a part-time teacher or scholar; it is also possible, given the right skill sets, to straddle applied and academic research and even move between consulting, government, and academic positions. The hope here is to offer some insights on how this might be accomplished under an assumption that the world of work will undergo changes (as has already happened in a dramatic fashion with the COVID-19 pandemic), some of which cannot be predicted.

Each of the authors (and many of their friends and colleagues) made the decision to not join academia, leave academia, or straddle the academic and non-academic realms for various reasons. A common thread though is that we have all had to figure out this path for ourselves, often in the face of stigma from within our respective fields. You might recognize some of this stigma. Sometimes professors push students into academia because they see this track as the most prestigious of pathways; their own reputation can be enhanced by the successes of former students. It is also sometimes the case that people embedded in industry might see former professors as not offering the greatest of value (consider needlessly pejorative phrases like "those who can't do, teach").

Our discussions with graduate students at conferences have made it clear to us that finding palatable work outside of academia remains an issue. We find that people also often wonder what we are doing there, not realizing that we can do research outside of academics. We, therefore, get questions about job basics, such as salary, sick leave, and working conditions, as well as more job-specific questions (e.g., "what is the difference between a contract and a grant?"). In the following chapters, we will address these questions and others. You'll face prejudices in different forms as you seek your own path; try to not let uninformed critics bother you as you seek out your own best circumstances.

1.4 GETTING THE LAY OF THE LAND – HOW TO READ THIS BOOK AND INTRODUCING ITS THREE AUTHORS

The primary focus of this book is on jobs in consulting, government, and research organizations external to universities,[17] though we also include information on starting and owning your own business. Throughout the book we address the following questions:

1. What types of organizations will hire me?
2. What types of jobs are there?
3. What are some typical basic characteristics of the jobs, such as salary, benefits, and schedule?
4. What is a typical career path like?
5. What are the typical duties?
6. What skills are needed?
7. What types of courses should I take?
8. How do I get these jobs?
9. What if I want to work for the government?
10. What if I decide I want to go into (or back into) academics?
11. What if I want to have my own business?
12. What if I want to work in multiple spheres?

The remainder of this book follows a natural flow, and it will make sense for you to continue with the next chapter and continue on through Chapter 10. However, each chapter was written to be read in a standalone fashion. A synopsis of the chapters is presented in Table 1.3.

The three authors of this book contributed to all of its chapters but given chapters were led by Stacey, Mercedes, or John. We also offer personal narratives or some fiction based on our narratives. Mercedes, for example, works at the National Institutes for Health so you'll not be surprised she has stories to tell when it comes to working in the government. We think you'll follow some of the stories a little better if you know something about each of our backgrounds; in Table 1.4 we offer a little more detail than what we offer in the author bios.

Table 1.3 Book Chapters Overview

Number	Title	Description
2	What types of organizations would hire me?	Provides an overview of the types of organizations that hire social scientists, the work they do, funding streams they tend to pursue, and thoughts about targeting these organizations for jobs.
3	What types of jobs would I be hired for and what are the typical tasks?	Discusses the types of jobs, responsibilities, and career paths that are typically available.
4	What skills will I need?	Presents the typical tasks performed and skills needed for these jobs. Predictions for skills needed in the near future are included.
5	How do I get these jobs?	How to get jobs outside of the federal government?
6	What if I want to work for the federal government?	How to get a job in the federal government?
7	What if I decide to go (back) into academia?	How to transition to academia either for the first time or returning?
8	What if I want to have my own business?	Having your own business.
9	What if I can't decide and want to do both?	Working in both academics and non-academics.
10	Can you give me any other help with my existential angst?	Summary, last pieces of advice, a pep talk, and a decision tree.

Table 1.4 Author Bios

Author	Background
Stacey	Stacey completed a Ph.D. sociology in 2001 with a concentration in research methods. In a quest to have greater work/life balance, during graduate school she decided not to go into academia. After graduate school, she was a postdoctoral fellow at the American Sociological Association, before commencing work at a research consulting firm. For about 10 years she worked at both large and small consulting firms, before starting a successful business in 2012. During the pandemic, she transitioned into a leadership role at a larger consulting firm.

(Continued)

Table 1.4 (Continued)

Author	Background
John	John completed a Ph.D. in 2003; he focused on educational psychology and research methods. He started out working for research consulting firms about a week after he defended his dissertation. After 5 years he obtained a tenure-track faculty position at Ohio University. He earned tenure there and then took a tenured position as a center director at Indiana University. During his entire time at Ohio University, he continued to consult with research firms and managed to translate most of these opportunities into published research. As a center director, John was formally a faculty member but he directed several staff and spent most of his time chasing and working on federal, state, international, and philanthropic research grants. This put John in a position to take on some compelling roles back in research consulting firms, where he started out. As of this writing, John has no specific plans to rejoin academia although he does miss teaching. If he did want to be a professor again, he's confident he could obtain a tenure-track position. Finally, John is a co-owner of a small publishing company; this might be a good semi-retirement gig.
Mercedes	Mercedes completed a Ph.D. in 2003. Her areas of focus included Latinx health, social epidemiology, and health disparities. After her postdoctoral training in nursing, she became the Director of Minority Affairs at a professional society in Washington, DC. As part of Mercedes' position as Director, she was to submit a competitive renewal for the Ruth L. Kirschstein Institutional National Research Service Award (T32) to the National Institute of Mental Health. Her National Institutes of Health (NIH) program officer at the time recruited her to NIH. This was over 15 years ago. Mercedes considers herself incredibly fortunate to work at a federal agency whose mission is to keep the public healthy through biomedical research and through a robust and diverse biomedical workforce. The views expressed in this book are those of Mercedes and do not necessarily represent those of the National Institutes of Health or the U.S. Department of Health and Human Services.

NOTES

1 LLC is an abbreviation for "Limited Liability Company." It is a kind of legal entity one creates to run a business, typically a small one, such as a hair salon, attorney firm, a publisher, consulting company, and so on. Formally, an LLC is a structure that combines characteristics of a sole proprietorship, partnership, and corporation and as the name implies it protects the owner from some personal liabilities. If you read that last sentence, really fast, it will sound like legalese you sometimes hear after a commercial!

2 Kroger, J. (2021, February 19). 650,000 colleagues have lost their jobs: Leadership in higher education. *Inside Higher Ed.* Retrieved May 19, 2022, from www.insidehighered.com

3 Zackal, J. (2021, February 21). Remote work is more of a possibility beyond the pandemic. *Higher Ed Jobs.* Retrieved May 19, 2022.

4 Reuters (941 Reuters – YouTube) (2020, June 3). Barack Obama joins virtual town hall to discuss police brutality (video). *YouTube.*

5 Dooling, B. C. E. (2020, May 12). *Agency learning agendas and regulatory research.* Brookings Institution Press. Retrieved May 18, 2022, from www.brookings.edu

6 American Association of University Professors (2018, October 11). *Data snapshot: Contingent faculty in US higher ed.* American Association of University Professors. Retrieved May 19, 2022, from www.aaup.org.10112018DataSnapshotTenure.pdf

7 Hartocollis, A. (2022, April 6). Help wanted: Adjunct professor, must have doctorate. Salary: $0. *The New York Times; UCLA wants to hire an adjunct: But the pay is zero. The New York Times.* Retrieved on May 12, 2022, from www.nytimes.com

8 American Federation of Teachers (2020). *An army of temps: AFT 2020 adjunct faculty quality of work/life report.* www.adjuncts_qualityworklife2020.pdf (aft.org)

9 Coser, L. A. (1974). *Greedy institutions: Patterns of undivided commitment.* The Free Press.

10 To be frank, one of the book's authors, John, fits this profile. He is a white male with a spouse willing to follow him through an academic career. Having made that point, as his career grew John landed a job in the Midwest, in a specific town where his spouse wanted to live. He and his family continue to reside in this town now that he works remotely.

11 We also don't want to give some of these books free advertising.

12 Flaherty, C. (2014, April 9). So much to do, so little time. *Inside Higher Ed.* Retrieved May 19, 2022, from www.insidehighered.com/news/2014/04/09/research-shows-professors-work-long-hours-and-spend-much-day-meetings

13 The "other social sciences" category includes American/U.S. Studies, Applied linguistics, Archaeology, Area, ethnic, and cultural studies, Criminology, Demography and population studies, Gender and women's studies, Geography, Gerontology (social sciences), Health policy analysis, History, science, and technology and society, International affairs/International relations, Linguistics, Public policy analysis, Statistics (social sciences), Urban, city, community, and regional planning, Urban studies/affairs, and General social sciences.

14 Thurgood, L., Golladay, L. J., & Hill, S. T. (2006). *U.S. doctorates in the 20th century.* National Science Foundation. www.nih.gov

15 U.S. Bureau of Labor Statistics (2020, April). Job market remains tight in 2019, as the unemployment rate falls to its lowest level since 1969. *Monthly Labor Review: U.S. Bureau of Labor Statistics.* Retrieved May 19, 2022, from www.bls.gov

16 Note that unless we specify otherwise, we treat Ph.D. as equivalent to other doctoral degrees (e.g., Psy.D., Ed.D.).

17 We recognize that there are research jobs at universities that might be considered as non-academic in nature; however, we do not address these types of jobs in this book. For example, during graduate school Stacey worked part-time doing institutional research in the financial aid office at her school.

Two

Doctorate holders (or advanced graduate students) searching for an academic job are typically familiar with being in a higher-education setting from years of undergraduate and graduate work. Though some institutions of higher education are more focused on teaching and others on research, there are common structures, organizational principles, and work environments that all colleges and universities share.

Non-academic organizations that hire social scientists can run the gamut from small nonprofits to large tech companies such as Amazon, Meta, and Twitter. Social scientists can also be found working for the government and government contractors. The options are quite varied, and the types of organizations will affect both the types of jobs available and the work demands. To make matters even more confusing, some organizations straddle multiple sectors in terms of services provided and funding sources. An overview of typical organizations that hire social scientists is presented in Table 2.1.

2.1 GOVERNMENT AGENCIES

The range of government agencies one can work for in the United States as a social scientist is quite broad. Aside from the federal government, there are also positions in state and local government agencies, as well as in other parts of the public sector such as school districts. The federal government, in particular, sponsors and produces research that would be cost-prohibitive for other types of entities such as nationwide and state-level large-scale data collections that can be used by other researchers. We cover working for federal government agencies in-depth in Chapter 6, though some of the principles will carry over into state and local government agencies.

2.2 GOVERNMENT CONTRACTORS

Government contractors provide goods and services to the public sector. We again have to point out that these jobs can be quite varied. Helping to

DOI: 10.4324/9780367815974-2

Table 2.1 Organization Type and Characteristics That Typically Hire Social Scientists

Organization Type	Description
Government	This category includes federal, state, and local governments, as well as other public sector entities such as school districts.
Government contractors	Primarily for-profit companies (though some contractors are non-profit entities) that sell goods and services to the public sector.
Think tanks	These are typically nonprofit, policy-research organizations, though some are located in the government. Some might be dedicated to advocating for a political ideology or a particular cause, though not all.
Consulting firms	These firms use industry expertise to identify and solve issues in other organizations. Though many of these organizations provide professional services to the government, they may also provide services to businesses in the private and nonprofit sectors.
General private industry	Other types of for-profit businesses such as curriculum developers, tech companies, pharmaceutical companies, and others that collect and analyze data.
Nonprofit and philanthropic organizations	Organizations other than think tanks created for reasons other than to make a profit, such as foundations, associations, and charities.

design airplanes to account for human factors and psychologists screening patients are both examples of government contracting gigs. At the federal level, about 40% of discretionary spending goes toward purchasing goods and services through contracts. For the fiscal year 2020, this amounted to $665 billion.[1] Of this amount, $243.3 billion was spent on services by civilian agencies, and of that $14 billion was spent on professional services which would include the types of research that social scientists might conduct.

2.3 THINK TANKS

Within Washington, DC, there is a cluster of think tanks, or policy research and engagement organizations[2] that comprise the so-called Think Tank Row, which includes some well-known organizations such as the Brookings Institution and the American Enterprise Institute; however, the organizations on Think Tank Row make up only a small percentage of think tanks in the country. According to the 2020 *Global Go To Think Tank Index*

Report produced by the Think Tanks and Civil Societies Program at the University of Pennsylvania, as of 2020 there were 2,203 think tanks in the United States, which was an increase from the prior year in spite of the COVID-19 pandemic, and more than double the number operating in the United States in 1980.[3] Think tanks are an example of an organization that can straddle multiple sectors of the economy and vary widely in characteristics, which has led to challenges in creating a precise definition of these entities. Existing in the realm between the public and private sectors and academia, think tanks may act as translators of academic research for use in policymaking, or producers of their own research.[4] The Civil Societies Program at the University of Pennsylvania classifies think tanks into seven categories based on their affiliation: (1) Autonomous and Independent, (2) Quasi-Independent, (3) Government Affiliated, (4) Quasi-Governmental, (5) University Affiliated, (6) Political Party Affiliated, and (7) Corporate (For Profit).[5] As James McGann notes, a key characteristic of all think tanks is that, unlike universities, they do not produce research for its own sake but in order to influence policy, and thus their products must be accessible to a wide audience.[6]

2.4 CONSULTING FIRMS

Consulting firms provide industry-specific guidance to help businesses and government entities address social problems and improve operations. They can conduct research within organizations to evaluate needs and use data to suggest recommendations. Though these firms may provide services to the government, they also have clients in other industries (and often serve as government contractors as well). The number of management consultants increased in the United States between 2012 and 2020 from 540,440 to 734,000, an increase of 36%.[7]

2.5 GENERAL PRIVATE INDUSTRY

These are for-profit companies for whom the government is not their primary client and are not consulting firms. These could be tech giants like Facebook and Google, health insurance companies, and curriculum developers. Dating sites and apps like Match.com and Tinder have social scientists on staff.[8] As the need for insights from data has expanded, so have the places where social scientists can find employment. The roles of social scientists in these organizations could be focused on interpreting user behavioral data.

2.6 NONPROFIT AND PHILANTHROPIC ORGANIZATIONS

As of 2016, there were 1.54 million nonprofit organizations in the United States comprising 5.6% of U.S. gross domestic product (GDP) according to the Urban Institute's National Center for Charitable Statistics.[9] Of these, over a third were human services groups such as food banks, family services, and homeless shelters (35.2%). The highest percentage of revenues (59.2%) were collected by health-related organizations, though they also had the largest percentage of expenses (60.3%), which would be consistent with the mission of being a nonprofit, where income needs to go toward expenses, versus profit.

Foundations represent another type of nonprofit organization; these can include philanthropic organizations. The Council on Foundations defines a foundation as "an entity that supports charitable activities by making grants to unrelated organizations or institutions or to individuals for scientific, educational, cultural, religious, or other charitable purposes."[10] As of 2020, there were 127,595 foundations in the United States, which gave away a total of $90 billion.[11] Of this total, 115,009 were independent foundations (90%). The areas that received the largest percentages of the grant funding were education (26%) and healthcare (23%).[12] As part of their mission, foundations may fund research related to the goals of the foundation, or fund evaluations of programs they have funded. They also may push for new ways of doing research. For example, the Equitable Evaluation Initiative was launched in 2019 by a group of foundations interested in developing evaluators with the awareness and skills needed to conduct equitable program evaluations (for a description of what an evaluator is, see Chapter 3).[13]

Readers of this book coming from an academic background are likely familiar with associations that in exchange for fees from their members provide various services such as advocacy for their membership at government agencies, professional development, conferences, and publications. These organizations often have their own internal research departments to conduct research on the memberships and trends in their field or in the broader society that are of importance to their membership. Some examples of these types of organizations are the American Association of Retired Persons (AARP), American Sociological Association (ASA), American Psychological Association (APA), National Education Association of the United States (NEA), and American Educational Research Association (AERA).

Larger nonprofits that provide direct services to populations also hire social scientists as part of the drive to conduct more internal evaluations and research that is relevant to the populations they serve. Some examples of these organizations are Meals on Wheels and Teach for America. Smaller nonprofits may not have enough money to hire someone permanently, though there are likely opportunities to volunteer to do some data analyses for them. One example of a volunteer program is the Washington Evaluators' *Evaluation Without Borders* initiative, where evaluators are paired with nonprofits to provide them with research support on a pro bono basis.[14]

To clarify a key point, there are jobs for people with doctoral-level degrees in all of these different sectors. Not surprisingly, it is important to study a different sector and understand how your current skill set and knowledge meet an organization's needs. A way to think about this is to imagine participating in a job interview for a position in a philanthropic group. If you can play that conversation out in your mind in such a way that you are describing how you can meet that organization's needs, then you're of course on the right track. But you likely cannot do this well until you understand key details like the philanthropy's mission and purpose, how it engages in the act of giving, its recent successes and drawbacks, and where leaders wish to take the organization in the immediate and near-term future. Through this book, we emphasize the need to know the different types of organizations, where you might seek employment and how organizations interact with each other.

For example, John works for a consulting firm that is a government contractor. Incidentally, when he was a university professor, he also provided consulting services and government contracting. Through these efforts, he has won grants with three large philanthropic organizations and he continuously seeks more of such opportunities as he pursues his research ideas. Furthermore, John works on federal contracts so he routinely interacts with doctoral-level staff who work for a U.S. agency. This means he's had to develop knowledge of how his specialty (education research) connects to his company's needs and the needs of funding sources. As a small-business owner, Stacey won contracts across different sectors – public, private, and nonprofit – by developing an understanding of the needs in these sectors and by marketing her skills to address the challenges unique to each sector.

The takeaway point here is that it is important to know your field, the different types of organizations in it, and the specific companies and philanthropies that influence the kind of work that goes on. Put another way, if you know just one area, and one type of organization, then that is where you'll likely find opportunity. If on the other hand, you know about a lot of different organization-types, then the field of opportunity for you will almost certainly widen.

NOTES

1 U.S. Government Accountability Office (2021, June 22). *A snapshot of government-wide contracting for FY 2020.* WatchBlog: Official Blog of the U.S. Government Accountability Office. Retrieved May 9, 2022.

2 McGann, J. G. (2021). *2020 global go to think tank index report: TTCSP global go to Think Tank index reports.* Retrieved May 9, 2022, from www.upenn.edu

3 McGann, J. G. (2021). *2020 global go to think tank index report: TTCSP global go to think tank index reports.* Retrieved May 9, 2022, from www.upenn.edu

4 McGann, J. G. (2016). *The fifth estate: Think tanks, public policy, and governance.* Brookings Institution Press.

5 McGann, J. G. (2021). *2020 global go to Think Tank index report: TTCSP global go to Think Tank index reports.* Retrieved May 9, 2022, from www.upenn.edu. Autonomous and independent think tanks are not affiliated with a particular interest group or donor, and are autonomous in their operation and funding. Quasi-Independent think tanks are controlled by an interest group, donor, or contracting agency, but autonomous from the government. Quasi-governmental think tanks are funded by the government, but not formally part of the government.

6 McGann, J. G. (2016). *The fifth estate: Think tanks, public policy, and governance.* Brookings Institution Press.

7 Statista Research Department (2022, May 2). Number of management consultants employed in the U.S. 2012–2020. *Statista.* Retrieved May 3, 2022, from www.statista.com/statistics/419968/number-of-management-consultants-us/

8 Ng, F. (2016, May 25). Tinder has an in-house sociologist, and her job is to figure out what you want. *Los Angeles Magazine.* Retrieved May 10, 2021, from www.lamag.com

9 The NCCS Team (2020, June). *The nonprofit sector in brief 2019: National center for charitable statistics.* Urban Institute. Retrieved May 3, 2022, from www.urban.org

10 Council on Foundations (n.d.). *Foundation basics.* Retrieved June 18, 2020, from www.cof.org/content/foundation-basics#what_is_a_foundation

11 Koob, A. (2021, June). Key facts on U.S. nonprofits and foundations. *Candid.* Retrieved May 18, 2022, from www.issuelab.org.38265.pdf

12 Koob, A. (2021, June). Key facts on U.S. nonprofits and foundations. *Candid.* Retrieved May 18, 2022, from www.issuelab.org.38265.pdf

13 Equitable Evaluation Initiative (n.d.). *About equitable evaluation initiative.* Equitable Evaluation Initiative. Retrieved May 3, 2022.

14 Washington Evaluators (n.d.). *Evaluation without borders.* Washington Evaluators. Retrieved May 3, 2022.

Three

Graduate students in social science Ph.D. programs are traditionally trained
to enter academia. The graduate experience provides both an apprentice-
ship experience (essentially on-the-job training) and a knowledge-building
experience. This training, coupled with close, often daily, interactions with
professors in the field yields the chance for students to become familiar
with the professoriate, yielding a relatively seamless transition to the world
of work as an academic.

However, the transition to non-academic jobs is often not so seamless.
This is because few graduate programs integrate their programs with
contract-based research organizations, government researchers, and philanthropies. It is of course possible to integrate consulting and other job
experiences into a graduate program, but doing so is generally contingent on grant-funded opportunities and graduate students need to
be assigned client-facing roles (we think such opportunities are rare).
Furthermore, such a setup would require purposeful, well-constructed
partnership between a graduate program and external business, philanthropic, and government entities, typically including a formalized internship program. This sort of partnership is, to the best of our knowledge, a
rare thing. Hence, graduate students typically are not afforded daily inter-
action with staff who work in non-academic organizations. This observation gets to the heart of this book: we wish prospective and current social
scientists to have a sense of the career options outside of academia.

3.1 TYPES OF JOBS

As stated in this book's introduction, there are a wide range of industries
that hire social scientists and the job requirements of starting positions will
correspondingly vary in scope and purpose. What these career pathways
have in common is that the first positions to be had are normally designed
to support research in some way. As one moves up through their career,
daily work typically moves toward making more overarching decisions
about research, client relations, and supervising junior staff.

DOI: 10.4324/9780367815974-3

It is common for early career staff to focus more on data collection and analyses, as compared to making major decisions around which grants to pursue and managing client expectations. As an example, when John obtained his first postdoctoral job in 2003, he worked on a large federal project that focuses to this day on research syntheses and meta-analysis. John spent his early days learning (and relearning) about meta-analysis and experimental and quasi-experimental design because in his last years of graduate school he focused more on mixed methods, ethnography, and psychometrics. He then spent much of his time coding studies, troubleshooting ideas senior staff developed and otherwise carrying out their vision, and carrying out analyses. It was probably a full year before he even met a client, and it was a couple of years before he was offering original contributions in client-facing meetings.

Similarly, Stacey had studied gender and work and family issues in graduate school, so she faced a steep learning curve when she made the move into educational research after doing a postdoc. Like John, for the first couple of years, she learned how to be a consultant and approached the experience with curiosity and humility as she learned a new field.

For those of you seeking a first job in consulting, be glad if you are offered a period wherein you can acclimate and develop knowledge valued by your employer. This acclimation process is important because you'll be working hard to read texts so that you are up to date in relevant research concepts. John was, for example, not familiar with the nuances of random versus fixed effects analysis (a topic that shows up in different forms of statistical modeling). Indeed, Stacey brought this up in a conversation one day with John and in short order John was reading up on the topic. This takes time and mental energy. What also takes time and mental energy is showing up to staff meetings being prepared and being capable of contributing. You'll want to think about meetings in advance. Ask yourself if you completed tasks you said you would handle in a prior meeting. If you successfully completed all tasks, be prepared to ask questions around the level of effort it took because supervisors need to calibrate staff workload projections. If you experienced challenges since your tasks were assigned, be prepared to describe them and make sure your supervisors are notified in advance so that they have a chance to help you. This is all mundane advice in a way, but some readers might be moving from a structured professional development model (e.g., graduate school) to a new environment. And one's supervisors might be dealing with a new project, and perhaps, a project that has not previously existed. Hence, you'll want to ensure that you take greater control of your learning because there is no syllabus to follow, and there is no five-chapter dissertation. This very much fits with an understanding of the "types of jobs" you might pursue because despite their variation, they all have one other thing in common other than working in a research support role: you're not being paid to be a student or to act like one.

3.1.1 Program Evaluation

One type of job is that of an evaluator (or program evaluator). The American Evaluation Association (AEA) defines the practice of evaluation broadly as "assessing the strengths and weaknesses of programs, policies, personnel, products, and organizations to improve their effectiveness."[1] We see evaluation as a type of research and there are permeable boundaries between the two concepts (e.g., there is research on how evaluations might be conducted or how research processes can be evaluated), and both use several of the same methods. However, research focuses more on theory building for the sake of generalizable knowledge, and evaluation focuses more on judging the merit or worth of some activity (sometimes for the purposes of improving it). Furthermore, evaluation is different from other types of social science research in that it is often the funder, program, or stakeholders that drive the research questions, rather than theory, though theory can and should be incorporated into the evaluation.

For purposes of understanding different careers, be aware that some people have strong perceptions about research and evaluation. Some clients might see research as some esoteric and abstract endeavor that might or might not yield practical and useful information. Other clients might scoff at the idea of conducting an evaluation because doing so is overly narrow and somehow not rigorous. Hence, it will benefit you to pay attention to key phrases like these and to explore how they are used in different organizations. We can spend some pages further delineating the matter, but this is not a book about evaluation or social science research; instead, we recommend that you (a) develop your own firm grasp of these phrases and other phrases in your subspecialty, (b) understand how prospective employers and clients see these terms, and (c) determine if you need to navigate any potential conflicts based on differing nomenclatures.

Evaluators can either work on *internal* and/or *external* questions. Internal questions tend to focus on whether the organization at which the evaluator is working deploys practices and/or programs that work as expected. Positions that focus on internal evaluation tend to be in organizations that offer products or services (either for-profit or nonprofit), and leaders of these organizations want to conduct internal performance checks. Such work is sometimes called formative evaluation, but a nuance here is that whereas formative evaluation typically focuses on program improvement, we mean to convey the idea that internal questions may focus more on organizational improvement potentially unrelated to a specific program, product, or service. Remembering this difference is not critical, what is important to know is that as an evaluator you might be tasked with focusing on improvement of processes and procedures because larger organizations often have the budget needed to keep a researcher on staff.

The prevalence of these types of internal evaluation jobs has expanded over the last 20 years and continues to do so. Previously, due to the costs of collecting and processing data, these jobs tended to be located in federal and state agencies that had the needed resources. These jobs have become more common as both data collection and processing have become more common, and there is an increasing demand to demonstrate effectiveness. For example, larger school districts now often have an internal research team, as do tech companies, pharmaceutical companies, and larger nonprofits.

By external questions, we mean research on topics outside of one's own organizational products, policies, or practices. Much academic research would fall into this category where the questions relate to topics or phenomena external to the university. Consulting, government contracting, and think tank jobs typically fall into this category where researchers are paid to answer questions related to national or local policies, help collect and analyze government data, or evaluate the programs, policies, or practices of other organizations. Stacey has, for example, plenty of experience leading external research dealing with improvement of student curricula, drug prevention programming designed for youth, and dropout prevention services, all while serving as a program evaluator.

3.2 TYPICAL TASKS

Many research tasks are similar across different types of jobs. These tasks might include:

- Developing an evaluation or research plan
- Understanding and helping to articulate program purposes through logic models and theory-of-change graphics
- Literature reviews
- Instrument design (e.g., surveys, interview protocols)
- Instrument pilots (e.g., testing interview protocols with a proxy sample)
- Data collection (e.g., conducting interviews, administering surveys)
- Data cleaning and collation (e.g., merging publicly available school data with data collected from a survey)
- Data analyses
- Writing report sections
- Editing report sections

To be clear, not all of these tasks will occur on each project you work on because projects vary in their scope. Clients typically will contract with your organization for a specific range of tasks that can be completed within a set timeframe and budget. For example, a client might contract with your organization to design an instrument, while another organization handles data collection, and yet another does the analysis.

Also, many end products will be in a different format than a traditional academic paper. This is because the audience for many products is not other academics but rather program stakeholders who may not have a research background. Similarly, some products are designed to provide information to the lay public who may not have any prior knowledge of the program or topic you are researching. Due to this, research products generally need to be more user friendly and writing should not be as academic in tone. Though some projects require a long technical report, there will also likely be a shorter, easily digestible product as well. As an aside, if you are good at taking complex prose and stating it simply, make sure you demonstrate this ability. Some in academia like to offer complex phrasing because they are either following some tradition, feel this helps communicate with their intended audience (typically, readers of specialty journals), or are just plain showing off. Hence, many words with a more academic flair are used in lieu of straightforward phrasing (e.g., utilize instead of use, iatrogenic instead of harmful) in an effort to appear to be in the clerisy (yes, we're trying to have some fun with irony here; clerisy means being in the intellectual elite, or highly learned). If you can make complex ideas accessible, you'll find steady employment as organizations pursue proposals and generate public reports.

There has also been an increase in a desire for "data-driven decision-making" which has compressed the timeline for results. Decision makers do not want to wait three years for research conclusions. They want real-time, usable information. There has been a corresponding increasing need for data dashboards, infographics, and mechanisms that allow report readers to conduct some of their own analyses. The organizations you work for will also want to promote your work, so part of your job may be to develop blogs and white papers based on your research. The bottom line is that your tasks will likely include creating research products that vary in format and tone from the traditional academic paper.

3.3 GOVERNMENT AGENCIES

We dedicate a whole chapter to working in the federal government (Chapter 6) because navigating the hiring system is notoriously challenging, and civil service laws make for strict occupation hierarchies. At the same time, there is quite a bit of transparency in terms of pay and duties. In the federal government, the extent to which you will be doing research or directing others to do research will depend on the agency and types of jobs. In some jobs you will be administering grants, and directing contractors; in others you might be conducting data analyses yourself. At the National Center for Educational Statistics (NCES), for example, due to budget restrictions on staff hiring, staff are primarily managing the work of outside contractors who do the bulk of the work of analyzing data collected and disseminated by the federal government.

State and local governments often have similar needs, though on a smaller scale. Hence, specific local government agencies might have their own research departments. For example, at school districts, staff may be conducting their own internal evaluations.

3.4 CONSULTING FIRMS

When trying to describe consulting jobs, Stacey has used the analogy of restaurants and caterers. Academics are like chefs who have their own restaurants. Chefs at restaurants design their own menu based on the meals that they are interested in creating, and customers go there for that style of food. Consultants, in contrast, are more like caterers, who can be great and creative, but create their menu interactively with clients.

With that in mind, there are three broad career pathways in large consulting firms:

- Project managers,
- Researchers, and
- Rainmakers/business development.

These are not mutually exclusive career categories, and to be most successful in consulting you'll need to do a combination of these tasks. However, in larger organizations upper-level managers will be engaged more in business development and broad project management, rather than day-to-day research tasks. This is to keep costs down but also because leaders should be working on developing relationships and exploiting them to develop market insights. This can be extraordinarily important in any kind of firm, but this might be especially true for consulting organizations. Think about this matter at a global level; a consulting firm needs customers, and these firms generally engage in contract-based research or technical assistance to carry out work that a government agency or philanthropy might not lead itself. Leaders of consulting firms therefore need to help generate business.

Returning to the catering analogy, any reader of this book might be able to operate as a caterer for their own event, but say the event includes about 100 guests. Think about the hassle of feeding 100 people while desiring to show a nice presentation, with servers, and then dealing with clean up (all while you might want to enjoy the event). All of a sudden, the idea of forking over the cash to a caterer might start to sound appealing. This becomes especially true if a caterer has insights on what foods are in-season, has access to specialty equipment (e.g., cutlery, dishware, tablecloths, buffet displays, chocolate fountains, furniture, and heating and cooling equipment), and can help customers envision the event. Do you want Italian fare to follow an appetizer with a massive charcuterie board? A buffet featuring Indian food? A seafood bake? Perhaps a boxed lunch? Caterers can work with customers to turn abstract ideas into concrete and specific plans with timelines. Now suppose a government education agency wants to improve the high school graduation rate in a state by reaching out to students who they know are on a path to dropping out. Just like a person might wish to reach out to a caterer before trying to offer a nice dinner experience for 100 people, the government agency might have broad ideas about how to use data to identify students who are at risk of school dropout and some approaches for helping those students who need it, but they do not necessarily have the in-house statistical skills needed to develop prediction models or up-to-date understanding around how to best help students who need support. Hence, they might issue a request for proposal to ask a consulting firm to provide support for the project.

This is where leaders in consulting firms can have special value. If said leaders paid attention to what the government agency has been discussing in public venues, then they might see what potential projects might be available in the future. To be clear, government agency staff should maintain a level playing field and not tip off to one contractor that a dropout prevention program will begin in a few months' time, while failing to tell others. But leaders in contract firms might be paying attention to state statistics, listening to what is being publicly stated in conference venues, reading any publicly available reports, and otherwise paying attention to trends. This is not very different from catering firms mining a database of public announcements of when couples get engaged and doing some advanced marketing in anticipation of a future wedding ceremony. Caterers are also likely attending to the natural timing of things (graduations tend to occur more in the spring; weddings have an uptick in the summer) and a consulting firm focusing on education will have a natural propensity to think about conducting research projects in ways that account for standard school calendars. Now consider that leaders in consulting firms will have a strong track record of carrying out research with a standard set of clients. These leaders know where clients congregate, have a sense of the material clients read, and otherwise try to make sure clients know they lead firms with a cadre of researchers. From there, if it seems likely that some states will begin to focus on dropout prevention, then the consulting firm should brush up on the high school dropout prevention literature and even reach out to professors and other experts in the field and engage in early relationship building. This is all a part of "rainmaking" and business development, and people who are good at it are worth their weight in gold.

The worth of a rainmaker is not just to the consulting firm. A person who is good at this work can offer critical services to the public because it can be quite difficult to guide thinkers from abstract ideas to concrete research projects that will yield usable results. The simple truth is that there are a number of public services that can be made more innovative, or at least efficient and it is so hard for any single person or even a group of people to see how to carry out big, important ideas. And sometimes it takes experience from one industry to inform plans in another. The person who can think like a caterer, but for a research consulting firm, plays an important role in helping society to roll along in a positive way (just like caterers who make it easier for people to celebrate graduations and get married).

Given that big picture background, whether stated explicitly or implied, in consulting firms, there is an expectation that you will contribute to business development efforts by either leading proposal efforts or writing sections of the proposals. Typically, you'll work on proposals as a part of a team, so you will not be shouldering the burden by yourself, but you should expect to engage in proposal development and sometimes lead generation proposals.

3.4.1 Project Management

Keeping a project on task and on time is one of the jobs of a project manager, as well as managing what is known in the field as "scope creep." When scope creep occurs, the project at hand evolves in ways where a client wants your organization to do more work than was originally in the contract. This is rarely if ever due to some underhanded and conscious effort to obtain free labor. A better explanation is that clients and contractors become excited about progress and possibilities that develop over the course of a long-term effort. There is a balance between providing extra value to clients to foster relationships and blowing a budget by doing extra work effectively for free. Such balance needs to be managed on a case-by-case basis. A good project manager will help in these cases, and in general a person in this role is critical for ensuring work is completed on time and within budget, contributing both to the success of the project and to the firm's reputation.

Now consider that project management is often intense, intellectually rigorous work when projects entail a large staff, interconnected timelines for project subcomponents, budget management and burn rates (i.e., the speed at which a firm is spending resources), and complex communications with a client, prospective and current members of a study sample, project leadership, project staff, and organizational leaders. Furthermore, project managers can rarely afford to not have a strong understanding of the research steps at hand. Be wary of the rare project manager who blithely states things like "I don't understand research" (and do not become this type of project manager yourself). It is important to understand the basic conduct of research steps so that a project manager can help the researcher think through timelines for tasks like literature reviews, item writing, piloting instruments, performing initial psychometrics, item revision, fielding, sampling, analyses, and report writing. Having made this point, researchers should take the time to explain component project steps so that a project manager can be maximally effective.

3.5 THINK TANKS

As discussed in Chapter 2, a wide range of firms can fall under the umbrella term of "think tank" though they all share a goal of influencing policy. James McGann argues that think tanks are structured in three primary ways: academic, contract research, and advocacy.[2] This is worth understanding because the type of think tank you work at will likely influence your tasks.

As described by McGann, academic think tanks are like universities without students and tend to hire staff with strong academic credentials. These institutions are focused on long-term policy goals, and their research can span a wide range of topics with the agenda determined by researchers and foundations. Contract research think tanks are more like consulting firms where they might develop relationships with a few government agencies that they work closely with and research agendas are developed in conjunction with the agencies. These organizations also tend to hire staff with strong academic credentials. Both of these types of organizations are known for conducting more objective research.[3]

Advocacy think tanks tend to be affiliated with a particular ideology, interest group, or political party. Staff at these institutions may not have as many academic social science credentials as the others, and the products are more likely to be policy briefs and white papers, than academic research papers.[4]

Whether the organization you work at is focused on short-term or long-term policy goals will also influence some of the work you do (though some of these boundaries are blurring). Short-term activities could include developing policy briefs and white papers, posting on social media, organizing and appearing at symposia, writing op-ed columns, and providing congressional testimony. Tasks at an organization with longer-term policy goals would include producing products more associated with academics, such as journal articles and books.[5]

3.6 PRIVATE INDUSTRY, NONPROFIT ORGANIZATIONS, AND PHILANTHROPIES

As data have become ubiquitous, it seems that there has been a parallel increase in the numbers of jobs available in private industry, nonprofit organizations, and philanthropies. Most of the jobs in private industry and nonprofit organizations would be dealing with internal research questions related to the effectiveness of products or services, or trends among "users." Most of this research is internally funded, removing some of the pressure for business development and grant writing. This does not preclude additional research though. Early in her career, Stacey worked in the research department of the American Sociological Association. Though the primary mission was to generate research briefs on trends in the membership and field of sociology, she did apply for and win grants to conduct additional studies.

When working in a philanthropy that is funding programs and research, you may not be doing as much primary research yourself but rather conceptualizing research areas to fund, and writing requests for proposals to garner applications from others who will do the research (similar to what Mercedes does in the government as described in Chapter 6). You may be providing technical assistance to grantees, guidance to potential grantees to increase capacity, and looking for overall trends in how your portfolio of projects is performing.

Given the range of tasks described, the range of skills needed in these jobs is broad. However, as discussed elsewhere you typically work in a team so you do not need to be strong in all areas. As discussed in the next chapter, you can bring a range of skills and interests to these jobs and still be successful.

NOTES

1 American Evaluation Association (n.d.). About the American Evaluation Association (AEA). *Values of the American Evaluation Association (AEA)*. American Evaluation Association. Retrieved May 11, 2021.

2 McGann, J. G. (2016). *The fifth estate: Think tanks, public policy, and governance*. Brookings Institution Press.

3 McGann, J. G. (2016). *The fifth estate: Think tanks, public policy, and governance*. Brookings Institution Press.

4 McGann, J. G. (2016). *The fifth estate: Think tanks, public policy, and governance*. Brookings Institution Press.

5 McGann, J. G. (2016). *The fifth estate: Think tanks, public policy, and governance*. Brookings Institution Press.

Four

Undeniably the skills gained during a typical graduate program in the social sciences are useful for non-academic jobs — otherwise these places would not hire people with Ph.D.s. Given that graduate programs differ in emphasis and that readers might be coming from a range of professions, in this chapter we discuss some of the typical tasks and skills needed for working in the consulting (including small consulting firms that are LLCs) and government arenas. One thing to keep in mind while considering jobs in these arenas is that fields are constantly evolving in response to changes in technology, policy changes, and cultural shifts. That is, what you work on might change based on client needs, so a flexible mindset and skill set, as well as a dedication to lifelong learning, will be helpful. For example, for a long time quantitative methodology was ascendent, though now with a greater focus on cultural competence and equity, mixed methods and qualitative data collection strategies are gaining more traction. In the field of education sciences, the use of a study design called randomized controlled trials (RCTs) was once rare. RCTs, which are in essence experiments, entail randomly assigning students, classrooms, schools, and so on, to two or more study conditions, typically to see if some new education intervention makes a difference. For example, one might randomly assign high schools either to use a novel dropout prevention program or to use normal efforts to prevent students from dropping out of school, all to see if the novel approach is more effective. RCTs of this nature were rarely used in education before 2005, but in the last 15 or so years they have become a widely used design because the federal government and other entities pushed to build the evidence base educators can draw from when making decisions about how to use their resources (e.g., whether to spend funds training staff to learn a new dropout prevention program).

More broadly, quantitative data was only able to become predominant due to increases in computing power over time. We have come a long way from working with data on punch cards and statistics dissertations

DOI: 10.4324/9780367815974-4

consisting of a regression equation with two independent variables because the calculations used to be done by hand. Back in the 1990s, when datasets were smaller, one might be expected to manage one's data along with developing the research questions and instruments. Data collection on individuals was also more limited to organizations that would conduct and fund surveys. Access to data-related careers was also more limited to those who had access to mainframe computers and training in statistical software that was often expensive to purchase. Now that datasets are much larger and organizations of all types are collecting and analyzing data, the range of quantitative data careers has expanded dramatically. There is free statistical software and people have easy access to powerful computers in their homes. Data visualization has become a field unto itself in that the aesthetics and accessibility of data presentation have become increasingly important as the need to understand data has moved from the halls of academia to the general public.

Computing advances have also impacted the work of qualitative researchers. There are multiple software packages that are used to organize textual, visual, and audio data (and so on) and support analyses. Indeed, what were once predominantly statistical software packages have now developed routines for qualitative analyses and some packages support statistical analyses of text data. This has led to a rise in methodologically oriented journals that focus on explaining how research might be conducted in lieu of focusing primarily on content.

Within this changing world, which may seem more and more dominated by computer scientists, there is a role for social scientists in guiding and interpreting research. There is of course a role for theory-based research. Also, there is almost too much data now, which can lead to the identification of spurious relationships. Social scientists can help focus the research. Providing technical assistance and increasing accessibility for all segments of the population is also an important role.

Given that technological changes will intertwine with evolving government priorities and policy foci, it is nearly impossible to predict specific skill sets that will be needed in non-academic jobs in the future. We may as well try to predict what so-called phones will be capable of ten years from now. Even if we were somewhat on target with our guesses about specific skills non-academic researchers will need, we'd have to admit to being lucky and hopefully the ideas in the book will be relevant even 20 years post-publication when the authors are flying their grandchildren to jet-pack training school.

Rather than prognosticating about skills, we suggest adopting a historical lens. There is nothing radical here. For example, most personal finance advice avoids making specific predictions about what the stock market will and will not do in the short term. Rather, one looks at historical market returns dating back more than 100 years to inform investment strategies. Architects and farmers consider long-term weather patterns to inform most of their practices (e.g., most homes built in Alaska will entail high-efficiency and redundant heat sources and bother less with air conditioning, and the reverse is true in Florida, all because of a sense of history). This is not always perfect and decision makers can rely too much on the past (see the 2021 Texas winter and how ill-prepared the infrastructure was for handling it), but this approach to pondering the future does have its merits.

4.1 HISTORICALLY IMPORTANT SOCIAL SCIENCE SKILLS

So what has a social scientist historically needed? In our experience, methodologies come and go. What have been constants so far are these capacities: (a) being able to learn, (b) writing and communicating, (c) planning/managing, and more broadly (d) thinking.

For many, if not most, social scientists in consulting, proposal work is the lifeblood of one's work. Contractors usually apply and compete for grants and contracts, and when they do so they typically develop a research proposal. Government and philanthropic workers offer requests for proposals (RFPs) and manage contractors who carry out projects on their behalf. Fortunately, most doctoral-level graduate students have a sense of a proposal via dissertation work.

So what is a proposal? John might propose to Mercedes and Stacey that he include a chapter in this book about a topic he really likes: Godzilla. He might do so because he thinks nuclear-powered ancient lizards that are as tall as a skyscraper are pretty cool, and he can use the concept of fighting Kaiju (that is a word for really big Godzilla-like monsters) as a metaphor for proposal writing. Stacey and Mercedes could in turn consider John's proposal, and likely turn him down. Simply put, putting forth a proposal is an act of asking others to consider an idea.

A research proposal is then simply a suggestion for how one might carry out a research project. Some proposals can be fairly short, simple, and straightforward; others can take weeks to months to prepare and cost companies tens of thousands of dollars in staff hours and other activities (e.g., travel) to generate. Whatever the size, most research begins with a proposal. Someone (e.g., a graduate student) proposes to do a project and others (e.g., a dissertation committee) consider the proposal and accept it, perhaps reject it, or oftentimes offer guidance on how to shape the proposal into something that is more refined and palatable. Anyone who has put together a proposal should immediately appreciate our historical lens for thinking about skills social scientists need (whether in academia or not), which again are: (a) being able to learn, (b) writing and communicating, (c) planning/managing, and more broadly, (d) thinking.

So here is some good news: even if your graduate training focused solely on preparing you for a career in academia at the expense of learning about other pathways, you at the very least have a sense of proposal activity and can translate this experience into needed skills outside of the professoriate. First, you need to learn to generate your proposal, and by now you should have a sense of how you learn best because sometimes you'll work on proposals that do not exactly fall within your bailiwick because even though you might not lead a project when rewarded, you still help work on the proposal. When this happens, you should also be reasonably accustomed to that disconcerting, but sometimes fun feeling of diving into a topic over which you have not developed full expertise. Then your proposal requires you to write and communicate (e.g., as in an oral defense). Postdoctoral proposals are almost universally going to require written arguments and plans, and sometimes a follow-along presentation. In our experience, a big change to postdoctoral proposal activity is that one must be able to communicate to non-technical audiences, whereas when we were in graduate school we felt compelled to show off technical prowess. Put less delicately, we were rewarded for sounding nerdy in graduate school, but after we graduated we had to learn to be more engaging and clear.

This point about communicating warrants a bit more attention. Proposals in the postdoctoral world are generally competitive efforts. It is not enough to impress a committee of professors with whom you worked and learned from over a few years; rather, you must impress other people who might never have met you, and you have to be more impressive than your competition. And regardless of whether they did meet you before, proposal scorers are almost always tired, harried, and worried about the fact that there is only enough funding for say one to two proposals, but there are dozens to be sorted out and ranked. All of this means that your proposal will typically not win by being good; it has to be great. It has to be better than the other proposals put together by other Ph.D.s who are motivated to conduct whatever research project. Hence, you will do yourself no favors by putting forth needlessly dense prose, or hinting that you do not really understand what a client wants. Your proposal has to be technically competent, interesting, and reflect a plan that will meet what a government or philanthropic entity seeks to accomplish. Collectively, the authors of this book have won millions of dollars in funded research activity via our proposals, but we have also experienced many, many losses. Furthermore, Stacey, Mercedes, and John have read and evaluated hundreds of proposals, and we know how hard it is to select finalists in a competition. Getting back to adopting a historical lens to prognosticate about skills social scientists will need in the future, our experience tells us that artificial intelligence or whatever will have to advance a long way before it replaces good writers and communicators. In sum, if you are able to

"Let's say you want to write an award-winning short story—you just push this key, here . . . "

Cartoon 4.1

Source: CartoonStock

communicate well within the social sciences, you will have work in any reasonable economy.

This does lead to planning and managing. Proposals (and later, actual projects) require good project management. Consider that very few people can convey complex ideas in writing in clear, easy-to-understand ways after a first rendering of text. Most proposals (and later, reports) need multiple rounds of thoughtful editing and writers who can embrace constructive feedback. Consider that a dissertation completed mostly by a student with a chair (i.e., a lead professor) providing pointers might be analogous to a marathon. The race is long; one needs endurance and a steady pace. Proposals and postdoctoral report writing in the industry is more like a relay race, with a baton being handed off from runner to runner to achieve an end objective. In this analogy, strong relay teams are skilled at hand-offs and some attention can be paid to one's running style. An explosive starter might begin the race; a compulsive and highly competitive runner who likes to be out front might be a finisher (i.e., an anchor). In many research organizations, proposals are written by well-managed teams if they are to win competitive grants and contract dollars. These teams are able to write subsections, meet deadlines, and pull pieces together in a coherent whole.

At the project phase, when one is performing funded work all of this applies as well except teams will not just focus on writing. Typically, teams have lead roles (e.g., project manager, principal investigators who offer content and thought leadership, data collectors, data analysts, writers, and financial budget control specialists). High-stake government research is almost always carried out by teams of people who can take the lead at different stages, much like in a relay race with a coach (similar to a project director) who watches performances and makes real-time decisions while everyone is cognizant of some clock/calendar. Similar to what we wrote about communicating, we think artificial intelligence will have to advance quite far before it might ever replace thoughtful project directors with good leadership skills.

This leads to the last capacity we listed: you'll need to be a good thinker in the consulting business. This observation is perhaps overly obvious, but hear us out. We want you to be prepared to succeed as non-academic social scientists. If for no other reason, when we are flying our grandchildren to jet-pack school, we'll feel a lot better if society is well managed by competent professionals. Your preparation requires that you understand that oftentimes your sphere of control will not be as wide as your sphere of responsibility. You might find that you have a great RCT plan but are having a hard time recruiting schools, teachers, or whatever because a pandemic hits and people become distracted from conducting research. Your funding might be cut down. It's a macabre and unfortunate point, but large research teams sometimes experience sickness or death among key staff members. We have seen or heard of research projects being undermined by:

- building fires,
- extreme weather events (hurricanes, tornadoes, floods),
- a pandemic,
- national economic turmoil,
- cybersecurity attacks,
- colleagues slipping on ice and needing medical care,
- inaccurate media coverage,
- changes in national leadership,
- and fastidious layers of editing somehow glossing over the word "public" missing the letter "L" in a title page.

The point here is research in the social sciences is rarely smooth and probably will not go as planned. Meanwhile, when you learned how to run stats in graduate school, you probably worked with pretty clean datasets and you certainly had syllabi to follow.

Over a long career you will need to think on your feet, and you will need to persevere through the unexpected if you want to be able to advance knowledge. So, by invoking this notion of being a good thinker, what we really mean to convey is not so much a cognitive attribute but an attitudinal one. Cultivate a sense that things often will not go as planned. You will run into challenges, many unforeseen, and so do not accept there is only one way to accomplish research. Some obstacles might be avoided, some can be smashed through, and sometimes obstacles themselves provide solutions.

An example is in order. John has been involved in a few RCTs. He pursued and won a prestigious grant that would not afford a budget where we could spend much on data collection. Without getting into too much detail, he went through a stretch where he did not think he could pull off the study the funder requested, and the funder was not in a position to provide more financial support. After much learning, communicating, planning, and thinking, John's team and the funder learned that outcome data (i.e., dependent variable data) were collected by a state agency. The state agency would not willingly release private, personally identifiable data on its citizens, but it was willing to release anonymized data that was just as good for purposes of the work. And this agency was happy to receive some accolades sent to a governor to help establish how the agency offers a benefit to citizens. This turned out to be a win, win. Having told this brief story, a skill set (or really a capacity) social scientists who perform applied research needs to have is the capacity to anticipate problems, adjust, and work through the unexpected. And this is as much an attitude as a cognitive process. One needs to control anxiety, have a thick skin, ask lots of questions, and be kind to oneself in this line of work.

This also means being patient with yourself and others. Depending on your personality, this is easier said than done. For many of us, practicing patience is like managing whatever vices with which you struggle (weight loss, alcohol use, obsessive thoughts, smoking, carrying grudges, binge TV, or whatever). That is, practicing patience is needed because you will be tested by miscommunication, egos (including your own), deadlines, competing priorities, technology glitches, health matters, and the neighbor's dog that will not stop barking all day but you never noticed back when you had an office. In our experience, practicing patience really is a skill and it must be cultivated.

Cultivating patience is important because for many research projects your sphere of responsibility can and will exceed your sphere of control. Try running a national survey project where you want hundreds of teachers to respond to some questions about their mathematics practices. Think about the challenges of recruiting 50 or so schools into a study and then randomizing them so that teachers might be exposed to one type of professional development or another. Then imagine following these schools for a year or two while trying to gather data and hoping not many staff change jobs. It is these types of studies that those of us in the consulting world and government contracts often find ourselves worrying over. The findings from these types of works can do much to improve policy and practice, and by extension the chance to conduct such research can be a great reason to get out of bed in the morning. But your *patience muscles* (again, with others and with yourself) will need to be strong; these muscles will need to hold a lot of weight.

4.2 IMPORTANT SKILLS IN THE NEAR TERM (POTENTIALLY)

Having made those points about the long term, we offer some shorter-term guesses about needed skill sets. As discussed in Chapter 3, there are quite varied types of roles in contract-based research and consulting and government work. In fact, the variation is such that most skills you would expect to see in the general business world will be valued in organizations dedicated to social science research. In a medium to large research organization, there is a need for leaders, analysts, sales, editors, writers, librarians, accountants, programmers, attorneys, contract specialists, administrative assistants, human resources staff, billing specialists, artists (and graphic artists), interviewers, report writers, and media personnel. If none of these roles sound appealing, then wait a while. New jobs emerge all of the time.

Of course, this book is pitched toward people who are seeking doctoral degrees (or already earned one). We will get into some thoughts about research skills shortly, but for now it is important to understand that there is a social science research variant to several if not all of the aforementioned types of jobs. The organizational executives we know (e.g., CEOs, presidents, vice presidents) generally have social science doctoral degrees. This is because they started as researchers, became project directors, grew into managers, and then went on to become organizational leaders. Most Ph.D.s in our experience do not follow this track because these roles are few in number, and frankly many of us are not overly fond of telling other people what to do. John was, for example, the director of a large research center for five years and at its height covered 20 staff. After that experience, he found that he does not mind leading a group, but he is not compelled to do so either, and he frankly finds it nice that some of the big decisions and problems leaders face are not his own. In contrast, we know others who just need to be the drivers; they want their hands on the steering wheel (i.e., they're happiest when being a boss).

We know Ph.D.s with visual art proclivities, and this comes in quite handy for data visualizations, client presentations, and otherwise communicating ideas. Consider skills like developing theory-of-change graphics and logic models with several component parts. If it is true that a picture can be worth a thousand words (and it is true) then the Ph.D. with an artistic bent will be welcomed in the world of applied research.

Speaking of a thousand words, are you the sort of person who likes to read directions for tax filing, technical manuals, or cross-reference paragraphs in ponderous tomes to make sure there are no inconsistencies? Chances are, the answer is no. But some readers will admit that this sounds appealing. If so, join the wonderful world of contract negotiation! There is so much here to do, and you get a chance to appease that inner lawyer (not the trial lawyer kind, the kind that is good at paperwork). In the contract world you get to deal with teaming agreements (e.g., agreements organizations make when they agree to partner on a large project), non-disclosure agreements, scope-of-work descriptions, and, well, contracts that range from a couple of pages to some fairly lengthy documents. In government contracting and research, you can even get into something called Federal Acquisition Regulation (FAR) clauses. Become good at this and you'll have tenure-like job stability!

If that last paragraph was depressing, then have no worries. You can take on a role like a Ph.D. salesperson. When writing proposals you might find you need to not only help craft the argument for why your ideas are better than the competitions' ideas, you can even work on developing "win themes." These themes are ideas that are put front in center of a proposal, and evidence in support of the themes is peppered throughout a document to remind proposal readers about why your organization and its approach is great. Want to be a show person? You might lead a sales presentation with PowerPoint slides, Prezis, videos, and so on to put on an effective argument for why you have a great idea and a great proposal. This means bringing sales energy, including a good ear for hearing a concern and an ability to quickly respond when needed, to address any concerns that a prospective client might have when trying to decide if you should be hired for the job. Similarly, you might be a staff person who is a go-to spokesperson when presenting to the media (e.g., newspaper reporters and television interviews).

Still not finding an appealing set of roles? Not a worry. There are social scientist Ph.D. variants of other job types previously mentioned: librarians, accountants, programmers, human resources staff, billing specialists, interviewers, and report writers. The roles are many, and it is also true that your career might lead you to try on several different hats.

4.3   JOB SKILLS AND RESEARCH METHODS

Now we jump into some observations about contemporary needs in research methods skill sets. See Table 4.1.

Table 4.1 Contemporary Research Methods Needs

Skill	Observations
Reading and Understanding Requests for Proposals	Request for Proposals (RFPs) can be quite lengthy and complex. If you want to be successful with your proposals, you'll need to, at a minimum, (a) read an RFP, (b) meet with others to discuss it, (c) read it again, (d) set up a proposal outline, (e) read the RFP yet again, and (f) then have it handy during the writing process. It becomes critical to do your level best to understand what a client wants, especially because proposal writing is typically a major, time-consuming endeavor and you do not want your ideas to be off base. If you can, review prior proposals that have been successful, and even proposals that were not. Finally, some competitions allow you to converse and even strategize with client representatives to help ensure that you develop the best possible proposal. Find out if this is the case because you will want to use every advantage that you can to win. It never hurts to ask if you can discuss a proposal with a potential client to help make sure you have a proper read and understanding of an RFP! One other trick of the trade is you should always request feedback on your proposal, especially when you do not win. This is generally not a fun activity, but figuring out why you lost can go a long way toward informing your next effort to win work from a client, and this will give you a better chance to make sure that you are reading future RFPs correctly.
Proposal Writing	A solid writer will likely never be unemployed. We social scientists do the hard work of translating research into actionable information via reporting, and one should never underestimate how challenging it can be to develop reports that are accurate and, hopefully, interesting. It is also important to know that there are different writing styles. *Proposal writing* requires some sense of sales and making a case for why your proposal should be funded. In this world, there is typically discussion of "win themes" that should be made plain in an introduction but then demonstrated throughout the remaining proposal. Writing tends to be active (i.e., limited use of passive voice that is often used in academic papers), confident, and you will want it to have some *pop*, meaning you are showing your understanding of why the work is important and your approach will do some good.

(Continued)

41   **What Skills Will I Need?**

Table 4.1 (Continued)

Skill	Observations
Project Management	Organized people who are accustomed to directing the work of others, developing timelines, Gantt charts, budget burn rates, and ensuring overall grant/contract compliance are worth their weight in gold. Organizations value experienced project managers, so much so that, if this sounds appealing, you might even wish to pick up a Project Management Professional (PMP) certification or at the very least make clear in your resume information about staff you led, if you helped projects be completed on time and within budget, and overall show that you're good at thinking through calendars and staff loads. Not everyone is good at this side of research so you'll find work if you can claim these abilities.
Qualitative Research	If you identify as a qualitative researcher, there can be opportunities for you in the applied social sciences. Qualitative research can be expensive but are at times highly valued to clientele because phenomena sometimes need to be explored and interpreted through some emergent theoretical lens. Program evaluation and other forms of applied research rely on interviews, document analyses, focus groups, and observations. Different forms of qualitative inquiry can be pursued as part of a mixed-methods study or as standalone (i.e., qualitative-only) research. Projects might entail interviews with research participants, leaders of large entities (e.g., school superintendents, hospital administrators), analyses of public and private plans (e.g., state public health plans), and observations of activities (e.g., preschool teacher approaches to behavior management).
	It is true that some funding entities tend to favor so-called quantitative studies (e.g., survey studies, RCTs), but there are nevertheless grants and contracts where a funder absolutely expects researchers to spend time with stakeholders and conduct qualitative work. And when these opportunities arise, Ph.Ds who understand qualitative design, analyses, and can budget out data collection prove to be of great value to their employer.

Research Design

Have you ever heard the phrase: "an ounce of prevention is worth a pound of cure?" Well, an ounce of research design is worth a pound of analysis (The authors of this book live in the United States, which inexplicably avoids the metric system. Hence, the prior quote can be stated as: "28.3495 grams of design is worth 0.45359 kg"). Applied research organizations, government or otherwise, need people who can set up design plans and help ensure those designs are followed during the course of a research project. An efficient design can save a lot of tears during the course of a project. Interestingly, some readers might assume that the same person who sets up a design is the same person who will run later analyses. This is sometimes the case, but not always. Some research programs can take a long time so the same personnel who are around at the beginning of a project are not always available at its end. It is also true that some people are better at different facets of a project. John might, for example, be good at conducting a priori power analyses and different approaches to randomization when conceptualizing an RCT, but he knows many a statistician who would be better at managing large datasets and conducting later impact analyses.

Data Management and Cleaning

These skills cover pre-analysis needs but are sometimes a form of analyses in their own right. There is almost always a need for people who can download data, transfer data across software packages, search for implausible values, deal with missing data (since this is the "real world," the data is almost always messy), and set up datafiles. Data management is an important skill set for large projects because many people might need to access a dataset and for different reasons. This means it is important to maintain a good quality codebook (i.e., variable description, how variables were constructed) and programming documentation that capture how analyses were run. Many forms of analyses entail component decisions (e.g., think of all of the steps that go into exploratory factor analysis), and it can be easy to forget important details from timepoints when data are collected, analyzed, reports drafted, and a client asks you to check some figure.

(Continued)

Table 4.1 [Continued]

Skill	Observations
Statistical Analyses	The vast majority of social science research requires a capacity for statistical analysis and an ability to learn new types of analyses as trends change. Analyses will range from simple descriptive work to complex modeling, depending on the research questions and data available. Stacey remembers how a lot of her time was spent on learning statistics and uses for various analyses in graduate school. In "the real world," after the research project was designed and implemented, and the data cleaned, this is often the fastest part of the research. An awareness of what analyses are appropriate for a given research question and data is important as well. Stacey does not use tobit and probit regression nearly as much as she might have thought she would but has used hierarchical linear modeling more because it is particularly applicable for analyzing data from educational settings.
Statistical Interpretation	There is always a need for sense making and figuring out what findings mean. Furthermore, there is a real skill to working with statisticians, programmers, and statistical programmers even if you are not one. Content experts will be needed to understand why some variables might be more important than others for a given analysis. Project directors and principal investigators are needed to ensure the right analyses are conducted, given the research questions at hand. Findings need to be understood in the context of theory.
Data Visualization	This is a hot topic right now. Advancements with software and web-based tools can make it much easier nowadays to tell a story with graphics, even interactive ones where an audience can pull together graphics based on questions of interest. For example, a report might describe the degree of racial segregation in school districts in a state by presenting a map that shows the density of students in minority schools in given areas, and the visualization might invite interaction by showing how the data change over a period of decades. Data visualization can require considerable creativity that must intersect with accuracy and being careful to not over-interpret a story, which can happen if graphics emphasize misleading details. How might this happen? Visual analysts have the power to persuade, and it is not unheard of for this power to be abused. Consider, for example,

how stock performance is sometimes used by some as clickbait. The next two charts show monthly S&P 500 performance and the top panel dates back to January 1985 and ends in October 2021. One can see a jagged but persistent rise in the index over the decades. This chart suggests that investing in the markets might be a good idea (hence the chart title). But when markets take a nosedive, as is the case in "The Sky is FallingChart!" a very different conclusion would be reached by the unaware consumer. Note that in this latter chart, we selected October 1, 2007, as a start and ended the date on February 1, 2009. That was indeed a painful time for the risk-averse investor, and we the authors of this book lived through watching our retirement balances drop. To make this look even more dramatic, we cut the Y (vertical axis) off at 700 for a low point, making the drop appear even steeper. From there, we formatted the shape to make it look even worse, even if the data themselves remain accurate. But for *as dramatic as this downturn was, it is barely perceptible in the main chart.* Our point? A visual depiction of these data is sometimes used to make some argument about a politician, sell some investment product, and otherwise manipulate emotion. We hope that any of our social science colleagues will use visual presentation skills responsibly, and be thoughtful about what stories to tell. (Note: consulting your financial professional for specific investing advice!).

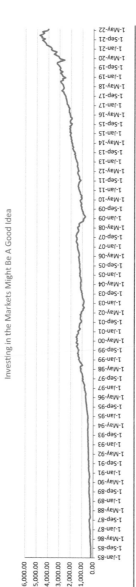

Investing in the Markets Might Be A Good Idea

(Continued)

45   **What Skills Will I Need?**

Table 4.1 [Continued]

Skill	Observations

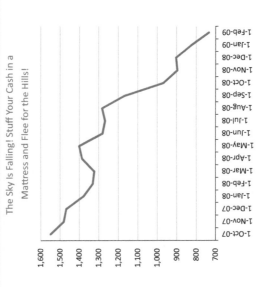

The Sky Is Falling! Stuff Your Cash in a
Mattress and Flee for the Hills!

Report Writing

Report writing differs from proposal work because you are transitioning from a description of what you will do if funded, to a description of what happened. Be aware that technical reports will differ from summaries/briefs, and the same information might be presented to a lay audience or experts who will provide a peer-review of your work. Some reports will focus more on advocacy (e.g., a report arguing the need for increased teacher pay and why this might save societal costs in the long run) and others will focus on "just the facts" so persuasion will be limited to convincing readers a study was well-conducted. Hence, thought must be put into the report type.

Explaining and Presenting

Being able to translate complicated topics for lay audiences or even educated audiences in different fields is a useful skill. Much of the work in non-academic jobs is conducted in multi-disciplinary teams where each of the participants may have jargon specific to their fields of expertise, so being able to find a common language and/or being open to asking questions for clarification is helpful. Being able to explain complicated, technical concepts in simple language is an important skill both for team building and for conveying to coworkers what you need to get your tasks done. Non-researcher coworkers may not understand the amount of work and thought that goes into data analysis and reporting. One sentence of findings may have hours of work behind it.

Research Translation

One point Stacey raises is that decades ago a professor told her that she thought of sociology as similar to astronomy in its impact – interesting but doesn't impact day-to-day life. In contrast, program evaluation jobs allow one to have a real impact on the world. Indeed, the guidelines of the American Evaluation Association indicate that we need to work toward a better society.

There has lately been renewed emphasis on describing the usefulness of research, particularly now with a focus on equity in research. Traditionally in academics, people present research to other academics and produce publications to be read by other academics. Though there will likely be others with Ph.D.s looking at your work, an equity approach to research means that the communities being studied have a stake in the research and the communities need to be provided with information. Though non-academic jobs have often emphasized a translation function of "research-to-practice," the practice was often still carried out by consultants. There is a movement now to empower communities with knowledge and increase their capacity. On a related point, if there is a research-to-practice gap, then in many cases we might look for the reverse of this idea: a practice-to-research gap. That is to say, there is merit in working with stakeholders to generate research questions, and using research to help people better understand issues and phenomena they care about. This can be seen by people who carry out so-called action research to address problems of practice, or sometimes localized problems. Importantly, some professors build their lab efforts/research agenda on this style of inquiry, but many faculty are still challenged to stake out their expertise and what they are known for so that they can build on the area. In other career fields, there is less of an emphasis for being known as one of the experts in some narrowly defined arena, and the social science Ph.D. will be more likely to conduct research on emerging needs and in applied settings.

In this chapter, we presented an overview of what skills non-academic social scientists have needed historically and will likely need in the near term. Again, we cannot completely predict the future (e.g., who would have predicted a few years ago that we would all need to be experts in how to use Zoom?), but have tried to give the best advice we can based on trends we have seen. Flexibility and a sense of curiosity about emerging trends will serve you well as situations change.

Five

Some of the questions we receive frequently about working outside of academia relate to the skills needed for non-academic jobs. What classes should I take? What types of professional development activities would be helpful if I am considering a career change? Are there certain topics I should read up on? In Chapter 4, we discussed the typical skills needed in these jobs, not all of which can be gained in graduate school. There is some on-the-job learning that will occur and is to be expected, though whether shifting gears in graduate school or making a mid-career change, there are things that can be done to ease the transition.

As an example, when Stacey was in graduate school and decided that she did not want to go into academia, there were few role models she looked to. Luckily, she had a supportive advisor and some professors had a policy focus, so there was some awareness about the requirements for jobs outside of academia among her mentors. Even so, there was feeling in the field of sociology at the time that anything "applied" was less prestigious (even though there was an applied focus among many of the early founders of the field) so after taking the required core courses in sociology, she took many outside of the department, including one in program evaluation which she loved. She had learned that quantitative skills would be highly transferable to jobs outside of academia so she took as many as she could and got a concentration in methodology. She enjoyed qualitative work as well and used both types of methods in her dissertation.

For some of these jobs, methodological skills are often more important than specific subject-matter knowledge. For example, job notices might indicate that qualified candidates can have a Ph.D. in a range of social science disciplines. As indicated in other places in this book, project teams can be made up of members from a range of disciplines, and the projects themselves can address a variety of topics (and the topics might change as administrations change), so it is the skills and flexibility to apply them in a variety of contexts that are important, more so than having a specific disciplinary background.

DOI: 10.4324/9780367815974-5

As with all things, there are trends in research where certain techniques and topics wax and wane in popularity in response to both changes in knowledge and technology, as well as societal trends. One example of this is the debates over the use of qualitative versus quantitative data. Prior to the advent of computers, multivariate statistical computations would have to be conducted by hand and so "quantitative" data analysis would be limited to summary statistics. Nowadays, qualitative data analyses also can be enhanced with computer software, making working with large qualitative datasets easier. For this and other reasons, the distinction between what we now think of as quantitative data and qualitative data is not as great.

Though in the mainstream press there is a lot of discussion about big data and data analytics, on consulting projects there is often a combination of qualitative and quantitative work to be done, so developing skills in both arenas can be useful. There are often exploratory studies and implementation studies that require a more qualitative approach to gain information about feasibility before a larger study is conducted. In addition, currently an increasing (and long overdue) interest in research equity has led to a push to incorporate more qualitative methods, with a mixed-methods approach gaining favor.

An important way to gain information on some of these trends and greater visibility in the fields you are interested in is through networking. Pre-COVID pandemic, physically going to professional conferences was important and this appears to be true during the time when society is returning to some pre-pandemic behaviors. Though going to presentations can be enlightening, making meaningful connections with other people in the organization happens through volunteering for positions. And your network is important! Associations always need people to review papers for their annual conference so volunteering to be a reviewer is an easy way to become involved. Go to the board meetings for organizations or interest groups you would like to work with and volunteer for positions. You might not become an officer right away, but working on a committee will help you make connections and get your name out there.

For better or worse, social media is an integral part of daily life for many people and should be considered as part of your job search strategy. LinkedIn, in particular, can be a powerful tool both for searching for jobs and for networking with people in organizations where you want to work. Recruiters also search on LinkedIn for potential job candidates. Indeed, John has used LinkedIn to recruit people who have specific skill sets and experiences, and otherwise stay in touch with people in the field because this platform does provide a handy way to network. It bears repeating that your social media accounts should be scrubbed for anything that might give a bad impression to a potential employer (delete those photos of you drunkenly riding backward on a horse). This is not to say that you need to be unidimensional. Indeed, depending on the outside interest, hobbies can demonstrate that you are a well-rounded person and volunteer work indicates that you are concerned about your community. People want to work with other people that are fun and interesting, but not a liability.

Social media can also help with the creation of your personal brand. Whereas in the past, branding was something associated with companies or products, now individuals are encouraged to work on their personal brand. Perusing LinkedIn profiles, many individual descriptions read like a personal mission statement, rather than their current position, or a description of tasks conducted in their current job. As people shift jobs more frequently and with the rise of the gig economy, individual careers become more like those of actors where they go from movie to movie, and they are hired for what they are known for. Careers become more about an individual's body of work, rather than a strict hierarchy of jobs where one gets progressively more responsibility.

When describing your body of work to potential employers, it is important to tailor your resume and cover letter to what is being looked for in the job announcement, as well as emphasizing skills that are generalizable across positions. The topic of Stacey's dissertation was leisure time, but she was able to get a job doing educational research and program evaluations years ago because she emphasized the skills she had learned and research techniques she had employed during graduate school when applying for jobs.

Another aspect of tailoring your resume to the job is to be aware that the first-level screen might be conducted by someone other than the hiring manager who is not as familiar with the skills you acquire through obtaining a Ph.D. The preliminary screen could be done by Artificial Intelligence (AI) or human resources staff that are looking for some key factors in order to move to resume to the next level. In Chapter 6, Mercedes describes how you should use keywords from the government job announcement in your resume to help make it through the screening process. Large companies often use AI to screen resumes so tailoring your resume to the announcement is important to getting your resume seen by human-resources staff.

Some other suggestions are to obtain an OrcID and create a Google Scholar profile. An OrcID is a digital identifier used to distinguish people from each other in the social sciences. If your last name is a common one (e.g., Wang, Smith, Li, Lopez), then you'll already have an uphill battle when tying your name to a given research report. If you have a middle initial, then use it (there are for example a few people with the name "John Hitchcock" conducting research). Adding an OrcID is however one of the best ways to ensure your research is tied to you and not someone else with the same or similar name. Getting an OrcID is easy; just search for the term on your favorite search engine and you can sign up quickly, for free. Once you establish your identity, consider building your profile on platforms like Google Scholar (there are other options). Google Scholar lists publications and papers you co-authored and includes metrics[1] like the number of times you have been cited, your h-index, and i10-index. The h-index is a metric that quickly describes the number of publications you author/co-author, and the number of times they have been cited: summarized as h articles with h citations. So if you authored five articles and each one has been cited at least five times, your h-index is 5. If you have five articles, four of them have been cited more than five times but one was cited four times, your h-index is 4. The i10-index is simply the number of articles (books, book chapters, etc.) that have been cited at least ten times. Building a Google Scholar profile is important in much of academia because research productivity is one requirement for tenure and promotion, but it can be helpful for social scientists working outside of academia as well because it offers a quick way to advertise staff. John was as you'll recall a professor for ten years and an adjunct professor for four years, so he was incentivized to build a profile; he has used it as an evidence point to offer prospective employers that he is adept at writing and completing reports so he'll often link his Google Scholar profile somewhere in applications and resumes. You might not end up building a large profile unless you're incentivized to do so, but regardless it helps to know what these indices are and why people sometimes report them even when outside of academia.

5.1 INTERVIEWS

After you get past the resume/job application screen, you'll of course reach the interview stage. This process can vary considerably on the basis of the style an organization follows. It is common to meet with several staff; these would be prospective coworkers, typically the person who will be your immediate supervisor after being hired, and often the overall leader of the unit that is hiring. You'll likely experience interviews that focus on different facets of your background. Some interviews will focus mostly on your research, others your methodological skills, and others your soft skills (do you seem likable, are you likely to communicate well with a client?). It is doubtful that this book can impart specific knowledge that you do not already have; we can only remind you that if you're being interviewed you are already valued. So it is okay and normal to be nervous during an interview, but you would not make it to this stage if you did not show strengths in your application process. And unless you're reading for an acting role, it is not the worst thing in the world if you get a little tripped up when communicating ideas. Take a deep breath and speak your mind knowing you belong even though you don't know everything there is to know about the prospective job (it's not your fault, you don't work there yet). Instead, try to keep in mind that you are likely not the only person being interviewed so you'll want to be prepared by learning as much as you can about an organization and thinking through how you can help its mission. Develop a narrative about how you can be a good fit and revisit it in different ways when answering the standard "why do you want to work here" questions.

One tip: if you are generally nervous about interviewing or find you are nervous about a particular interview, one way to prepare is to conceptualize the questions you will likely be asked. Write these questions down, and develop your responses. Consider conducting a mock interview with some colleagues or a friend and role play until you feel pretty confident in your answers. And if in the interview you're hit with a knowledge item and you do not feel confident in your answers, remember to at least say that you're a researcher and accustomed to ambiguity and learning new concepts (i.e., I might not know the answer now, but I'll figure it out because I'm good at research!).

It is common to be asked to offer a "job talk," which is a presentation about your research and research interests. Polish your PowerPoint (or Prezi, or whatever) presentation and work to tell the story of your research. Describe why the work interested you in the first place; this will go a long way in helping others to be interested. Describe challenges you experienced and how you overcame them, moments of success and reasons why you deserve some credit, how you persevered through it all, and why the findings mean to a lay audience. Be sure to understand parameters like presentation time, time you should leave for questions, topics and angles that are likely to be of greatest interest to your prospective colleagues, people who will likely attend your talk, and make sure you have a chance to test run and troubleshoot any equipment. You might be presenting on-line or there might be an on-line audience, so make sure you are ready for these formats. For example, if you're presenting via an on-line meeting format like Zoom, check to make sure your background looks good even if you plan to use background settings, make sure pets and children will not interrupt you, and so on. If you're presenting in person, but audience members are on-line, be proactive in talking to them and make it clear that you are trying to include them in the process.

We do think that we can offer some advice that you might not already know about, which is how to handle the interview stage when you're asked if you have questions. You should always have a few questions and these will differ on the basis of whether you're interviewing with a consulting firm, a small business, a think tank, or a government agency. And your questions, when well-crafted, can simultaneously show you learned a lot about your prospective employer while putting you into a position to learn new information. Some general topics to consider when engaging in background research about an organization:

- What is its purpose and mission?
- What are its major activities?
- How large is it?
- How long has it been in existence? Is there any evidence that it is financially stable?
- Has the organization undergone noticeable changes (e.g., did it acquire other organizations, was it itself acquired, is the organization boasting of some recent, major win)?
- Is there evidence the organization has a high staff turnover rate? If so, why? Is the turnover rate low?
- Do leaders appear to be grown from within, hired from without, both?
- What other entities compete and/or partner with the organization with which you are interviewing?
- What are the career paths described on an organization website?

Take a look at the benefits package as well; this is of course something you need to know to understand a later compensation package, but a benefits package sometimes signals organizational values and goals. If, for example, an organization has a generous tuition reimbursement program, unusually competitive health insurance packages, strong support for transportation for a physical office versus strong support for remote staff, then you might glean some insights about your potential employer and future plans. Look for anything that stands out and you might have fodder for asking questions in the interview that are much more informed. Compare these two questions: "tell me about your benefits package" (which really is best suited for human resources recruiters) versus "I see that you offer expansive tuition reimbursement programs for staff in the management track, does this mean you plan to grow your future leaders from within?" (and this question might be posed to a unit lead). Overall, by learning about an organization by asking the types of questions presented in this section, you'll be in a position to develop sharp questions to present during the two-way street known as the interview. You might, for example, observe that a group is led by a highly experienced and long-standing team. This should be comforting and you might note this, but knowing this can also open the door to asking about plans to groom a future generation of leaders.

These last set of questions should apply to any given type of organization. Some other questions to investigate before an interview and used as fodder to ask well-targeted questions during the interview will differ somewhat based on organization type. For example, if you're interviewing with a small firm, it is fair to gently ask about financial stability, its longevity, the firm's exact niche, and what would ever happen should the niche change. For consulting firms, consider its niche position and if this fits with your skillset. Most firms can cover all standard research methods, but some firms might be known for survey work, others for conducting randomized controlled trials, and yet others for qualitative inquiry. Consulting firms also will vary with respect to topical/subject-matter experience and expertise. Whereas one firm might for example have an excellent track record in studying, say, teacher turnover, other firms might boast leading expertise in special education inquiry. You should learn about a firm's market position and ponder if you are being recruited to strengthen an existing skill set (e.g., if you're a survey specialist joining a leading survey research firm, or if you are a survey specialist being recruited to join a company less known for survey work.) With that comparison between your expertise and a consulting firm's specialty, you'll be able to make keen observations during the recruiting process, ask keen questions, and overall present as a much stronger candidate.

If you are interviewing with a think tank or philanthropy, you'll want to pay special attention to organizational mission and purpose. You should always peruse a company's recent reports to get a feel for their work, but it becomes especially important to carefully consider your expertise, and attitude, relative to a specific ideological framework. Ask yourself, how can you advance the group's purpose and mission? What is the societal benefit of your research and how does it fit in? These sorts of questions generally entail complex answers so you can ask about these matters in an interview, but show you've engaged in some initial thinking, at least enough to establish that you had good reasons to apply for the position at hand.

Applying for government jobs and how to best handle the interview process warrants a separate chapter, which we turn to next.

NOTE

1 As is the case with most phenomena, do not let your impressions of a person's scholarly productivity be dictated by a few numbers. Sometimes majestic works go unnoticed for long periods of time, and other works are cited often because they are criticized. Similarly, you might see students with lower GPAs who took classes they found to be personally challenging, and other students who stuck with coursework that they found to be easy.

Six

Just like academia or consulting, working for the federal government is not for everyone. Yet the federal government offers great opportunities to social scientists who want to apply their skills in the "real world." As discussed earlier, perhaps during graduate school, you were persuaded to think that the academic job route was the only path. After all, what else could a person who writes a dissertation, publishes papers, teaches courses, and presents at conferences do? As you have already learned from reading this book, there are a lot of jobs social scientists can hold outside of academia; this includes the federal government.

Some federal agencies are more natural places for social scientists to work at (i.e., United States Census Bureau, Centers for Disease Control and Prevention, Agency for Healthcare Research and Quality, Substance Abuse and Mental Health Services Administration, and Centers for Medicare and Medicaid Services); however, there are others that might not readily come to mind (i.e., U.S. Secret Service, Department of Agriculture, and U.S. Department of State). Contrary to some of the messages you might have received in graduate school (Mercedes got them too!), life outside of academia can be intellectually rewarding. A social scientist's responsibility within the federal government will vary. Some positions might call for you to conduct research, publish agency-specific reports, or manage a scientific research portfolio. These positions will offer you growth opportunities for both your skills and interests.

Like academic positions, federal jobs require analytical, critical thinking, and writing and oral presentation skills. In fact, depending on the federal agency, social scientists contribute to the intellectual enterprise in the form of developing publications, funding opportunities to advance a scientific area, convening panels of experts to judge scientific merit of grant applications, and writing federal reports, just to name a few. A major difference between the academic world and government is that there is no tenure process; however, the federal government offers job security and stability.

DOI: 10.4324/9780367815974-6

Like many before Mercedes, after she completed her Ph.D. and post-doctoral training, she "hit" the traditional academic job market, did the job talks, and even had job offers. However, she knew early in graduate school that an academic life was not for her. She had no interest in teaching. She liked research but did not want the pressure of writing grants. She also knew she wanted to keep learning about areas of science outside of her own. In order to please her mentors, she applied for academic positions, but also positions in the "real" world. Specifically, she applied to a nonprofit. That initial nonprofit job is what led her to the National Institutes of Health (NIH). She knew about NIH because her mentors received funding from the agency and working there intrigued her. She thought to herself, why not go where the money is?

As a Program Officer and Section Chief, her day-to-day routine varies; however, the bulk of her job involves helping investigators navigate the NIH grant funding ecosystem. She spends hours speaking with investigators (on Zoom) about funding opportunities, and the many in-and-outs of the grant-making process. The best part of her job is working with budding investigators who are full of ideas and are trying to transition to the next level in their career trajectory. She also helps shape the state of science by writing Funding Opportunity Announcements. Typically, this means keeping current on the state of the field. She also gets to manage people.

Working in the federal government is not full of rainbows, gummy bears, and unicorns. Despite the many positive aspects of her job, there are some less pleasant duties. The most unpleasant aspect of her job is when she has to deliver bad news. The bad news can come in the flavor of "your research doesn't fall within the mission of the Institute;" "your grant received a good score, yet we don't have money to fund you;" and "your science is important, but it is incremental in nature and not transformative enough." Second, she also does not have self-autonomy. There is a chain of command in the federal government that must be followed. The chain of commands includes asking permission to publish or to volunteer for an activity. Third, as a federal employee, there is information she cannot share. Managing knowledge – knowing what is for public consumption versus what is not – is part of being a federal employee.

Entry into the federal government has a number of on-ramps, and the key is finding an on-ramp that is appropriate for your career phase. This chapter aims to provide you with tips on how to navigate the federal government job search, what the application process looks like, what to expect, and information about alternative on-ramps onto the federal government workforce. The target audience for this chapter is individuals "early" in the career trajectory. The guidance offered is not comprehensive nor should be seen as the end all be all of "how to." Mercedes does not work in Human Resources (HR) or have working knowledge about the hiring practices across the federal government. Rather, her goal is that you will know more about the federal government's hiring process than she did 15 years ago when she applied for her first federal job.

6.1 TIPS FOR GETTING STARTED

Unlike the private sector, the hiring timeline in the federal government is long. Federal agencies are required to announce, rate, rank, interview/assess, and investigate applicants before selections are made. The hiring process can vary by government agency; however, the journey begins with an USAJobs.gov posting. This is the website where federal jobs are posted and houses the application portal. As an applicant, you will need to set up an account in order to apply and upload any application materials. Knowing which federal agency is of interest narrows the job search. Mercedes knew that she wanted to work at the National Institutes of Health (NIH), so her job search, on USAJobs.gov, was incredibly focused. Despite the focused job search, it took her two years to get her first federal job.

Why? She really did not know what she was doing. Mercedes had not done her homework. She had not done any preparation work to aid her in the application and certification process. Overall, Mercedes had no clue what the application, interview, and hiring process looked like. She had a super shallow understanding of the mission of the NIH Institutes and Centers. She did not know how to read a job posting. She also had no understanding of the federal government pay scale. Her luck turned when she met someone who worked at NIH who helped her to navigate the process. In the next section of the chapter, Mercedes offers some tips on how to get started and make it through the certification process so that your resume is seen by a hiring manager. These tips are based on things that she did not do; so you can learn from her mistakes.

6.2 TIPS FOR MAKING IT THROUGH THE CERTIFICATION PROCESS

6.2.1 Resume/Curriculum Vitae (CV)

The certification process is a step that entails ensuring you have the basic qualifications required for the advertised job opening. We are sure you have been advised many times (as Mercedes was) to customize your resume/CV. Believe it or not, Mercedes consistently failed to customize her resume to match job announcements. She was guilty of thinking that her resume/CV was strong and competitive enough. Unfortunately, this was not the case. A common pitfall is that the resume/CV does not match what a government resume should look like. The government resume/CV has to be written in a particular format and style, which may make it longer than traditional resumes, and also distinct from what you would submit for an academic job.

There are some key elements to a federal CV which include, but are not limited to, your contact information, citizenship status, if relevant the highest General Schedule (GS) grade,[1] veterans' preference, list of work experience, and education and degrees. The contact information is standard, and something found in regular resumes. However, citizenship status is perhaps an information item not included on an academic CV. If U.S. citizen status is required for the job posting, by including this information you are aiding the hiring official (verification of citizenship status comes at the time of hiring).

Federal resumes require detailed information of your work experience over the last ten years. Just like other resumes, noting your professional experiences, especially in positions related to the job you are applying

"I'll have to get someone younger to look at
your résumé. I'm not fluent in emoji."

Cartoon 6.1

Source: CartoonStock

for, at the beginning of the CV is prudent. For those who lack significant professional experience, you may want to consider listing your education first and choosing the most applicable positions that prove you are suited for the job. While disclosing veteran status is not required, this does tell a hiring official more about your work experience. The bottom line here is to provide the most detailed account of your qualifications and work experiences:

- Employer's name and location
- Job title
- Start and end date: If you are currently employed, use "present" to indicate that you still work there
- Average number of hours worked per week
- Detailed description of daily responsibilities: Where appropriate, use key phrases from the federal job description to highlight your relevant experience and skills required by the position
- Awards or special recognition
- Supervisor's name and contact information

Similar to other resumes, make sure to include each school you have attended, and any degrees received. Additionally, when appropriate include if you have any specialized training outside of work experience or education; volunteer work; fluency in languages other than English, professional affiliations; publications on subjects that are job-relevant; and any other additional skills that are relevant to the position. The key is to focus on quality versus quantity that directly speaks to the position. Finally, feel free to list references. Provide the name, contact information, and relationship for each reference. Professional references such as current supervisors, former coworkers, professors, and mentors are all appropriate.

Once you have a well-crafted CV, then it is important to further customize it by incorporating keywords from the posting. This is because artificial intelligence can be used as a way to vet resumes. With this in mind, if the job announcement calls for planning of scientific meetings, then your CV should reflect that you have the knowledge, skills, and abilities to successfully achieve that.

6.2.2 GS Pay Scale

The GS pay scale is the predominant pay scale for federal employees, especially employees in professional, technical, administrative, or clerical positions. The GS scale goes from 1 to 15 with 10 steps within each grade; a position listed at 1 or 2 generally requires a high school diploma and little experience. A GS-5 typically requires a bachelor's degree and a 9 usually requires a master's degree; a new Ph.D. is often able to seek work in Grades 11–12. Grade band salary ranges change on an annual basis and the federal government makes adjustments for locality. An employee working in Washington, DC, will earn more than a colleague at the same GS working in, say, Evansville, IN, to account for different cost of living expenses for each city. Given this variability, we do not list all salary ranges in this book (a few salary ranges that are current as of this writing are described later); the information however is easily found on-line.

A common reason an applicant is found "not qualified" is that candidates apply for positions above their knowledge, skills, and abilities level. Each federal position falls within a pay band on the GS pay scale. The position on the pay band is classified on the basis of historical expectations of the work. The historical expectations include, but it is not limited to, the scope of work, job knowledge, job requirements, abilities, responsibilities, complexity, skills, management related tasks, etc. The resume/CV and the assessment questions are intended to evaluate your ability to perform the historical expectations of the work.

The GS scale has a predetermined pay increase at each step. If you have never held a federal position, list your annual salary in your CV. This will be used to gauge your salary on the GS scale. However, an interested candidate has to be realistic in their expectations of where they might fall in the GS scale. Recent Ph.D. job candidates, without postdoctoral experience, are likely to start at a lower GS level than someone with postdoctoral experience. Recall that a recent Ph.D. might begin as a GS-12 or lower, depending on experience. Mercedes' lack of knowledge of the GS and being realistic about where she might pass the certification process is a major reason why she did not make a number of certification thresholds early on. She wanted a higher salary, but often her lack of work experience meant that she did not meet the requirement for a higher GS posting (GS-13, GS-14, and GS-15).

6.2.3 Informational Interviews

Each federal agency, division within an agency, and position will have its positives and negatives. It is your job to find out what these might be. Reaching out to individuals in the agency you want to work at and conducting an informational interview can help you learn the "positives" and "negatives" of an agency, division, and position. The informational interview can offer you a perspective on the mission of the agency, the kind of work that goes on there, and the hiring process and practices. In all honesty, it never occurred to Mercedes to schedule informational interviews.

Scheduling informational interviews is easier said than done. Whenever possible, Mercedes tends to remind junior investigators that people are willing to help. People enjoy talking about their favorite subject – themselves. More senior-level professionals are always willing to offer sage guidance about career choices. Schedule a 30-minute informational interview and ask individuals to tell you about what they do. How did they get there? What do they love about their job? What aspects of their job do they like least? This is your chance to get curious, listen, and learn. If needed, schedule another 30 minutes. This will give you an opportunity to ask follow-up questions. Please do not forget to send them a thank-you note after each informational interview. This speaks to your level of professionalism and your ability to close the loop.

How might you find a few federal employees to reach out to for an informational interview? Similar to the recommendations for networking for other types of jobs, one likely place to meet and engage with federal employees is your disciplinary scientific annual meeting. Federal employees attend scientific meetings. Federal employees are members of panels, present posters at poster sessions, attend section business meetings, etc. You might be one or two degrees of separation from a federal employee through your current network. Your mentors and professors might have colleagues or former students who are federal employees. Your mentors and professors can also help. They can introduce you to these individuals or suggest individuals with whom you can speak with. If a federal employee authors a report or a manuscript that you find interesting, this provides you with a perfect opportunity to write to that person, introduce yourself, and ask for an informational interview. After the informational interviews, take the time to revisit your CV with fresh eyes. There might be things that you learn from the informational interviews that you might want to incorporate into your CV.

Next, we focus on how to read and digest job announcements found on USAJobs.gov; there are a few key informational pieces to look for and about which to be mindful. One item to consider is the number of days the job announcement posting you are interested in has been active. The number of days the job announcement is active will vary. As an applicant, it is important that you keep this in mind. You do not want to miss the closing date. Next, you should know where the job posting falls in the GS pay scale. You do not want to apply to a job announcement that is higher than where you can document you have the knowledge, skills, and abilities. Figure 6.1 shows an example of these key features. The posting is open for five working days and falls within the GS 9–11 (salary ranges currently between $61,947 and $97,430), respectively. Third, know the locality of the job. In this case, one position is open in Montgomery County, MD. However, the government has federal offices and job opportunities across the country. If you want to live in the Washington, DC, region, then a position in Montgomery County, MD might be for you. However, if you are looking for a job in Maine, then this job opportunity might not be for you. The example noted in Figure also shows how many positions will be filled. In this case, there is one (1) position open for this posting.

Next, government job postings also provide information about for whom the announcement is intended to hire. I will use an NIH job posting, as the next example (see Figure 6.2). At NIH, two parallel announcements are often posted for positions – one for non-federal employees and one for federal employees. The job announcement shown

Open & closing dates
🕐 02/03/2022 to 02/07/2022

Salary
$61,947 - $97,430 per year

Pay scale & grade
GS 9 - 11

Location
1 vacancy in the following location:

📍 **Montgomery County, MD**

Figure 6.1 Position Open & Closing Dates and Pay Scale and Grade

in Figure 6.2 has been modified from a real NIH job announcement – NIH-GR-DE-22–11453968. The job announcement number is not included in Figure 6.2. When reading an announcement like NIH-GR-DE-22–11453968, the NIH part of the announcement number indicates which agency posted the opportunity. The letters "DE" designate that the posting is open to the public – individuals outside of the government – and military spouses.

The parallel posting (see Figure 6.3) – NIH-GR-MP-22–11453969 – is intended for individuals within the federal government. Just like

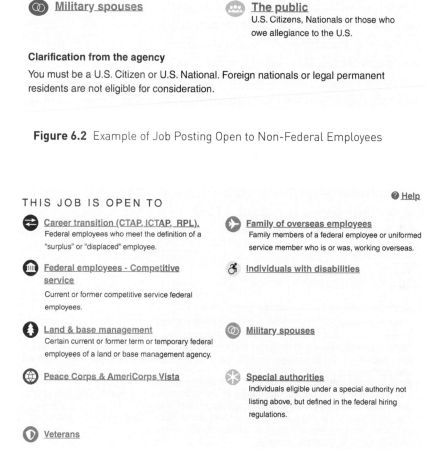

THIS JOB IS OPEN TO ⦿ Help

⦿ **Military spouses**

⦿ **The public**
U.S. Citizens, Nationals or those who owe allegiance to the U.S.

Clarification from the agency
You must be a U.S. Citizen or U.S. National. Foreign nationals or legal permanent residents are not eligible for consideration.

Figure 6.2 Example of Job Posting Open to Non-Federal Employees

THIS JOB IS OPEN TO ⦿ Help

⇄ **Career transition (CTAP, ICTAP, RPL),**
Federal employees who meet the definition of a "surplus" or "displaced" employee.

✈ **Family of overseas employees**
Family members of a federal employee or uniformed service member who is or was, working overseas.

🏛 **Federal employees - Competitive service**
Current or former competitive service federal employees.

♿ **Individuals with disabilities**

🌲 **Land & base management**
Certain current or former term or temporary federal employees of a land or base management agency.

⦿ **Military spouses**

🌐 **Peace Corps & AmeriCorps Vista**

✳ **Special authorities**
Individuals eligible under a special authority not listing above, but defined in the federal hiring regulations.

➊ **Veterans**

Figure 6.3 Example of Job Posting Open to Federal Employees

before the NIH part of the position announcement number indicates that the hiring agency is NIH. The "merit promotion" in this posting indicates that the position is open to federal employees, spouses of military members, Peace Corps and AmeriCorps individuals, and family of overseas employees, just to name a few examples. If you, as a candidate, submit an application that fails to meet the requirement for whom the job is open to, then the system will find you ineligible. You will be automatically eliminated from the pool of candidates. This means that you will not be considered, and your name will not be forwarded to a hiring manager.

Another component of federal position posting is that it includes a description of the duties to be performed. Next is an example of the kinds of duties that might be mentioned on a job posting (Figure 6.4):

When evaluating if the job announcement is right for you, please pay attention to the duties that are required and revisit your CV to ensure you have the knowledge, skills, and abilities to perform the job. Your CV should corroborate that you can successfully execute the duties.

Next, each job announcement includes qualification information. Under this section of the announcement, there will be details about the educational level, specialized experience, or combination of these two that is required for the GS levels. The higher the GS level, the higher the bar for qualifying for the position. Figure 6.5 shows the required NIH qualifications for candidates at the GS-9 level, compared to at the GS-11. As Figure 6.5 shows, a GS-9 candidate does not "need" a Ph.D. or equivalent doctorate degree. In contrast, a Ph.D. is often required at the GS-11 level. It is important to read this section carefully and to understand any

Duties

- Implement administrative functions for the office.
- Keep supervisor fully informed of current conditions throughout the organization and take appropriate action to ensure that administrative activities are properly implemented.
- Provide administrative and technical support, compiling and preparing information and documentation, and assisting in making logistical arrangements as required for meetings and conferences.
- Analyze organizational programs and activities through review of reports and initiate or recommend action to correct problems and improve programs. Evaluate, process, and make recommendations for effective organizational changes.
- Assists supervisor in the coordination of tasks and duties of subordinate staff within the office, ensuring that the administrative and clerical functions required for a smooth and efficient operation are provided.

Figure 6.4 Example of Duties in Federal Job Posting

Qualifications

In order to qualify for a Staff Assistant position at the GS-9 level, you must have:

A. completed a Master's or equivalent graduate degree, or 2 full years of progressively higher level graduate education leading to such a degree or an LL.B. or J.D., if related;

OR

B. 1 year of specialized experience equivalent to at least the GS-07 level in the Federal service obtained in either the private or public sector, performing the following types of tasks: *identifying procedures required for the completion of an administrative project; responding to inquiries concerning organizational projects and activities; and distributing and drafting responses to internal and external correspondence;*

OR

C. a combination of post baccalaureate education related to the position and experience that meets 100% of the qualification requirments for this position.

In order to qualify for a Staff Assistant position at the GS-11 level, you must have:

A. completed a Ph.D. or equivalent graduate degree, or 3 full years of progressively higher level graduate education leading to such a degree or an LL.M., if related;

OR

B. 1 year of specialized experience equivalent to at least the GS-09 level in the Federal service obtained in either the private or public sector, performing the following types of tasks: analyzing administrative problems, developing recommendations, and synthesizing the data into reports or briefings; implementing administrative functions for an office; and coordinating with internal and external stakeholders on administrative matters of interest;

OR

C. a combination of post baccalaureate education related to the position and experience that meets 100% of the qualification requirments for this position.

Do not copy and paste the duties, specialized experience, or occupational assessment questionnaire from this announcement into your resume as that will not be considered a demonstration of your qualifications for this position.

You will receive credit for all experience material to the position, including experience gained in religious, civic, welfare, service, and organizational activities, regardless of whether you received pay.

Preview assessment questionnarie before you apply:

https://apply.usastaffing.gov/ViewQuestionnaire/11327065

Figure 6.5 Information About Candidate Qualifications

experiential or educational position requirements. If you accidentally apply for a GS-11 position without a Ph.D., then the system will find you ineligible for the position. However, the opposite is not true. If you have a Ph.D. and you apply for a GS-9, it is possible that you will be found to qualify for the position.

If you plan to apply for a position that requires a Ph.D., we recommend that you dig up your graduate school transcript and submit it along with your application materials. Not all positions require candidates to submit their transcripts, however, some do. Transcripts offer important information. They indicate the highest degree you earned, hence documenting your highest educational attainment. Transcripts also show the coursework you completed, the grades you earned, and (sometimes) the title of your dissertation. There are some positions for which you might not have enough work experience, yet your educational attainment (validated by your transcripts) will show that you meet the qualification for a position. Even after 15 years of federal service, Mercedes still uploads her graduate school transcripts, just to be on the safe side.

Figure 6.6 is from a Program Analyst job posting where the job announcement includes a section that specifically references how educational attainment can be used in lieu of experience.

Each job announcement also provides you information about "How to Apply" for the position. The "How to Apply" gives some step-by-step guidance, and it tells you the time the posting expires. In this case 11:59 PM ET on 02/05/2020 (See Figure 6.7).

Now let's move on to what happens after you enter the application portal, and you upload your CV into the system. The next step is to address some assessment questions. The submission of your transcripts comes at the end of the application process.

6.2.5 Assessment Questions

As part of the application process, you most likely will be required to answer a series of assessment questions that correspond with the duties of the position. This is an additional way Human Resources (HR) determines if you have the knowledge, skills, and abilities for the position. The assessment questions often asked you to choose the statement from a list that best describes your experience, training, or ability. The assessment questions collect information about you to see if you are an expert on a task, through education and experience, and gauge if you have a comprehensive and authoritative knowledge of or skill in a particular area.

Education

If you qualify based on education in lieu of specialized experience, you are strongly encouraged to submit a copy of your transcripts or a list of your courses including titles, credit hours completed and grades. Unofficial transcripts will be accepted in the application packages. Official transcripts will be required from all selectees prior to receiving an official offer. Click here for information on Foreign Education.

Figure 6.6 Educational Attainment as a Way to Qualify for a Job Announcement

How to Apply

To apply for this position, please read and follow all Instructions in this announcement, complete the online application, and submit the documentation specified in the "Required Documents" section. Your complete application package must be submitted by 11:59 PM Eastern Time (ET) on 02/05/2022 to receive consideration.

1. **To begin, click Apply to access the online application.** You will need to be logged into your USAJOBS account to apply.

2. **Follow the prompts to select your resume and/or other supporting documents to be included with your application package.** See the "Required Documents" section for any additional forms and/or supplemental materials required.

3. **Read all Eligibility questions and respond accordingly to any Eligibility you wish to claim.** You aill only be considered for those Eligibility questions (Status Applicant, Reinststement, Schedule A, etc.) you respond in the affirmative to, regardless of what documentation you submit. We cannot assume you intended to respond differently to a question based on other information in your application package.

4. **Complete the assessment questionnaire.** Applicants are asked all questions regardless of their consideration preferences. We will only consider you for the grades, series, locations, specialties, and other considerations that you self-identity as being qualified for or interested in. Preview assessment questionnaire before you apply:
   https://apply.usastaffing.gov/ViewQuestionnaire/1135-1186
   (https://apply.usastaffing.gov/ViewQuestionnaire/1135-1186)

5. **Verify all required documentation is Included in your application package,** review your responses to the assessment questionnaire for accuracy, and then submit your application.

In addition to the required documents, **we encourage you to submit a cover letter, copy of your transcripts, and any applicable certifications or licenses.** Even though this information is not required at the time of application, we may request this information later.

Figure 6.7 "How to Apply" Guidance

A common error in this phase of the process is when candidates do not read the assessment questions carefully. Please read the questions multiple times to ensure you understand what is being queried. The system allows you to start the application and return to finish at a later time; this flexibility can, of course, be useful but sometimes candidates can lose their bearing and this can yield bad outcomes. As an assessment question might ask, "Are you a U.S. citizen?" And you accidentally click "no." If U.S. citizenship is required, by clicking "no," the system will automatically deem you as "not qualified." Let us drill down a little on the types of assessment questions you might see.

- Do you possess a bachelor's degree, or graduate/higher level degree with major study in an academic field related to the medical field, health sciences, or allied sciences appropriate to the work of this position? (This degree must be from an educational program from an accrediting body recognized by the U.S. Department of Education at the time the degree was obtained.)

The answer options might be written as a "Yes" or "No."

If you click, "yes" then your transcript will confirm this information.

Other assessment questions might ask you about your experiences in, for example:

- Identifying areas of progress, opportunity, and relative need
- Analyzing and monitoring developments in a given area and how it related to an organization's programs, policies, and legislation
- Identifying existing changes or developments in a given area/field
- Identifying existing and emerging areas to resolve programmatic problems
- Interpreting scientific information to develop papers or written testimony for non-scientific audiences
- Coordinating team activities
- Writing reports, evaluations, summary statements, and corresponding as a part of the peer-review process

Response options might look like this:

- I have not had education, training, or experience in performing this task.
- I have an education or training in how to perform this task but have not yet performed it on the job.
- I have performed this task on the job. My work on this task was monitored closely by a supervisor or senior employee to ensure compliance with proper procedures.
- I have performed this task as a regular part of a job. I have performed it independently and normally without review by a supervisor or senior employee.
- I am considered an expert in performing this task. I have supervised performance of this task or am normally the person who is consulted by other workers to assist or train them in doing this task because of my expertise.

The assessment questions aim to ascertain competency, knowledge, skills, and abilities. Competencies are the attributes required to perform a job and are generally demonstrated through qualifying experience, education, or training. Knowledge is a body of information applied directly to the performance of a function. Skill is an observable competence to perform a learned psychomotor act. Ability is the competency to perform an observable behavior or a behavior that results in an observable product.

Depending on the agency you applied to, the system might let you know, via email, the outcome of the certification process. However, it is possible that your application will enter an information abyss. Yes, this is incredibly annoying and frustrating. Unfortunately, be prepared to never hear back!

6.2.6 Human Resources

Government job announcements may have an HR contact name, email, and/or number. The HR contact person can help candidates navigate the application process and address questions. Mercedes regrets never calling HR to ask why she did not make the "cert." She should have, but she never did. Depending on the federal agency, your behavioral science degree might fall within a particular Office of Personnel Management classification. The job classification has implications for the kind of positions you might certify for and promotion potential. The HR person assigned to the posting can offer you practical guidance about how your skill set and experience match or do not match the job posting. You do not want to spin your wheels by applying to a position that is above the GS level for which you are qualified.

Federal agencies provide reasonable accommodation to applicants with disabilities. If you need a reasonable accommodation for any part of the application and hiring process, contact the HR contact on the vacancy announcement. Candidates are to reach out to the HR contact before the closing date of any job announcement of interest.

On the basis of your CV and the way you addressed the assessment questions, HR staff will decide if you qualify or not for the position. Typically, the system notifies you, via email, if you made the certification process or not (but again, you might need to be proactive and check). Applications are reviewed and applicants are certified by pre-defined "quality categories." The "quality categories" fall in three buckets: qualified, well qualified, and best qualified. Recall that Applicants found "not qualified" do not make the certification or "cert." This means that the applicant was found not to have knowledge, skills, and abilities required by the position. If you fall in this camp, your name will not be provided to the various hiring officials.

6.3 DECISION POINTS AFTER THE CERTIFICATION PROCESS

6.3.1 First Decision Point: Candidate's Resumes/CVs Are Reviewed

Hiring officials, after the certifications are available, are able to see the names of individuals who serve as a pool of candidates for the various open positions. This pool might include a robust list of individuals from which to pull candidates. Hiring officials often look for candidates whose CV matches key characteristics. For example, if the hiring manager is looking for someone with certain kinds of analytical skills, then the hiring official might search for candidates who have those particular skills. This takes an enormous amount of time.

Once the list of candidates has been identified, either just the hiring official or a small team is put together to identify the top candidates to invite for an interview. A hiring process Mercedes was involved, which consisted of her boss and her pulling candidates from the "cert." Her boss was part of the hiring part of the process; she vetted every CV. They were looking for candidates that not only had the experience to success-fully execute the tasks associated with the position, but the candidate had to have skills, knowledge, and abilities that complimented the entire team in the Division.

6.3.2 Second Decision Point: Interview Process

The interview process varies and there is no one way of doing interviews. The interview process will vary not only by agency, it will vary by depart-ment, by position, and by level of position. For example, there might be an interview with one person who might "screen" you – potentially the person who would be your supervisor. This person might then refer you to a panel. The panel might be a panel of three or five. In some cases, the interview will include the person who would be your supervisor, followed by an interview with their chain of command (higher ups). In contrast, the interview might mirror an academic job talk. That is, you will be invited to spend the whole day meeting with a number of individuals, similar to what is described in the chapter that describes job talks conducted to pursue positions in consulting firms. The day could start with a meeting with the person who would supervise you, one-on-one meetings with the Division/Section Chiefs, a one-on-one meeting with the Division Direct (and Deputy Director if one is part of the chain of command), a group meeting with key people in the organization, a group meeting with your potential new peers, and a one-hour seminar. This kind of interview pro-cess is exhausting for both the candidate and the group doing the hiring.

Hence, only a short list of candidates is forwarded to people like Mercedes and her supervisor, who also interviewed the candidates.

Hiring of new staff has been active during the COVID-19 pandemic and the pandemic might have led to long-standing changes in the processes used by some federal government agencies. Thanks to technology, Zoom has made it possible for interviews to be conducted on screen – face-to-face – and for job seminars to be given. Certainly, a job seminar via Zoom can present some challenges, but it is possible. As a reminder, please dress professionally/business casual for any Zoom – informal and formal – conversations with any person from the agency you want to be hired. This will show a level of formality and seriousness that might resonate with some of the individuals you speak with. Your potential supervisor will ask for feedback from everyone who interacted with you during the interview process. You want to be memorable in positive ways.

The types of questions you will get during the interview will depend on the position and where it falls on the GS scale. If the position calls for specific technical skills, then the interview questions are likely to reflect that. Let me highlight some of the common interview questions:

- Tell me about yourself (keep this to about 5 minutes). Share about the skills you bring to the job while telling them a story about you.
- Why do you want to work here?
- Why should we hire you?
- Please talk about your experience working with different teams and skill sets.
- Describe coming to a new situation and you need to get up to speed quickly, what do you do to learn the position? What support might you need?
- Can you describe a situation when a task outcome was not clear? How did you manage this situation?
- Describe your perfect job.
- What are your strengths and areas for improvement?
- Why did you leave (or want to leave) your current position?
- Tell me about an unpopular decision you made that put you at odds with your supervisor.
- Describe your efforts in the Diversity, Equity, Inclusion, and Accessibility space.

- Managerial positions: Tell me about your experience managing people.
- For analyst positions: Can you please discuss your data analysis experience and in particular, your experience with unstructured or semi-structured data?

On your end, have a few questions for those who are interviewing you. Often candidates forget that the job searching process is a two-way street. The hiring organization evaluates you for fit, but you are also evaluating if the job is right for you. In addition to asking about the next steps and timeline for hiring, candidates might want to ask:

- What are the most rewarding aspects of your job? (a question for peers)
- Were there internal candidates for this position? (a question for peers/supervisor)
- What was the telework culture here before COVID-19? (a question for peers and supervisor)
- How are new employees onboarded? (a question for peers and supervisor)
- Who are the stakeholders? (a question for peers and supervisor)
- What are the deliverables and expectations for the person hired say in the first 100 days? (a question for a supervisor)
- How would you define your leadership style? (a question for a supervisor)

After the interviews, send a little thank-you email to everyone with whom you interacted – from the person who scheduled the interview to the highest-ranked individual who took the time to meet with you. If you do not have access to their contact information, ask the person who interviewed you to forward your thank you email as needed.

6.3.3 Third Decision Point: Selection Process

The selection process from the federal employing agency can take time. The employer not only revisits and assesses CVs of interest but also gathers information related to the interview. As a hiring official, Mercedes takes notes of responses and observations. Her notes include comments about what made the candidate memorable – both positive and negative. Typically, candidates are ranked, and then HR is notified about which candidate should be extended an offer. Often the person who will be your supervisor might reach out to inform you that you have been selected for the position. However, an HR official is the only federal entity that has the authority to make a formal offer.

As a candidate, you too get to assess the interview and job process. During the interview, as a candidate you should get a feel if the position at hand is a good fit for you. The position, the agency, and the atmosphere should be right for you. Do of course take the time to be reflective if this is where you see yourself in both the short and long terms. Mercedes has turned down jobs at the time when HR reaches out to her. At times she has asked for her candidacy to be removed from the process when she has been asked to provide references. Some of the reasons she decided to step away from opportunities stemmed from her perception of "fit." She did not think she wanted to work in a particular environment. Turning down a job is within your purview. You want to be somewhere where you can grow professionally and personally. Not every position and place will be a fit.

Reference checking is part of the process. If you make the short list, you will be asked to provide three references. Your potential new supervisor will call the individuals whom you provide. They might have a standard set of questions that will be posed to your referees. Here too, be mindful about whose names you provide. Ahead of time, ask the potential referees if they would be able to provide a positive reference. Not all referees do. We have known of hiring officials who use social media to learn about you – another potential "reference." As described in prior chapters, please be mindful of what you post on social media and if need be scrub your accounts.

6.3.4   Job Offer and Onboarding

As a reminder, HR is the unit that has the authority to make job offers. An HR representative can address questions about your starting GS grade and starting salary. As a candidate, you have three options when an offer comes. You can decline the position, accept it, or offer a counteroffer. If the starting salary offered by HR is below what you are currently paid, then you may want to enter into that discussion with the HR. If you enter into a salary negotiation, the HR official is most likely to ask you for additional documentation.

The onboarding process can include a background check, drug screen/physical, relocation (if applicable), and paperwork related to benefits. Depending, where you are hired, that Division/Office might also have an internal onboarding process. The agency onboarding process often includes the issuing of equipment, welcome gatherings, 1:1 meetings with your supervisor and peers, and so on.

6.4 ALTERNATIVE ROUTES TO ENTERING THE FEDERAL GOVERNMENT

In addition to USAJobs.gov, you can consider applying to a fellowship that can serve as a stepping stone toward a federal position. In this section of the chapter, we describe some of these opportunities.

The U.S. Department of Health and Human Services (HHS) sponsors the next generation of leaders who might join the federal ranks and support the overall mission to serve the U.S. public through the HHS Emerging Leaders Program. The HHS Emerging Leaders Program is a competitive, two-year, paid, federal internship within HHS. The program provides interns with a unique opportunity to develop enhanced leadership skills in one of the largest federal agencies in the nation. The program provides an excellent opportunity for participants to begin a professional career in HHS.

The Presidential Management Fellow (PMF) Program is currently[2] another path to federal employment. This program is a two-year program designed to attract early (1–2 years out from graduate school) advanced degree candidates. The program is administered by the U.S. Office of Personnel Management and the application process for this program is rigorous. This fellowship program appears on the USAJOBS website. Finalists of the PMF program are pre-qualified at GS-9 level. Agencies can hire individuals at GS-9, GS-11, and GS-12.

Another opportunity is the American Association for the Advancement of Science (AAAS). The Science and Technology Policy Fellowship (STPF) provides opportunities for outstanding scientists and engineers to learn first-hand about federal policymaking while using their knowledge and skills to address pressing societal challenges. STPF Fellows serve yearlong assignments in the federal government and represent a broad range of backgrounds, disciplines, and career stages. Many AAAS Fellows successfully transition from this fellowship to federal service. This is a great way for interested individuals to get their feet wet and make a good impression on the agencies and offices to which they are assigned.

The Robert Wood Johnson Health Policy Fellows program is a residential fellowship experience in Washington, DC. This opportunity is for mid-career professionals. The goal is to prepare individuals to influence the future of healthcare and accelerate their own career development. Fellows actively participate in the formulation of national health policies in congressional offices and accelerate their careers as leaders in health policy. Fellows are able to continue their health policy activities for up to 12 months after the Washington placement period.

Many federal employees begin as contractors. There is a range of Federal contracting agencies. One example is Kelly Government Solutions; however, there are many others. Recall that federal contractors are not federal employees and different rules apply for each type of employee. However, contractors get to work side by side with government employees and pick up skills that are important to various positions. Contractors are often in a good position to be competitive for federal jobs. In addition to picking up skills, contractors learn about the hiring process at the agencies in which they are providing a service.

Let us reassure you that things can turn out ok so long as you persevere. You are on the path that you are supposed to be, and it is normal not to know exactly what might come next (we do not know what the future will bring for us either). Since you are reading this book, this indicates that you are open to options, and you are willing to chart a course that feels right for you. If the federal government is where you want to work, then that is simply wonderful. Remember to plan ahead and do your homework. The federal government works slowly. Seek out people who might be able to assist. See your missteps as opportunity points that can bring you successes in unexpected places.

NOTES

1 The GS is described later in this chapter. For now, it is sufficient to know that it is a classification and pay system used for civilian, federal employees.

2 This program and others described in this book are subject to change. The important takeaway to keep in mind as this book becomes aged is to find similar program types.

Seven

Despite rumors to the contrary, professors change jobs. They, for example, change universities, often for personal reasons or sometimes to pursue appointments at what they see as more prestigious institutions or programs. Some professors move into administrative roles. The typical pathway is to move from serving as an assistant professor by obtaining tenure and the rank of associate professor, later become a full professor, then become a department chair. From that point on, one can potentially become a dean, be it an assistant dean, full dean, or otherwise. Some deans, of course, move on to become university provosts and presidents. Of course, some professors leave academia completely. This might be because they were not awarded tenure after a given period of time; usually, they have about seven years to establish the academic profile (informed by research, teaching, and service) their colleagues expect to see before awarding tenure and promotion. If faculty are not awarded tenure, they typically move on to other roles. Regardless of their tenure status, some professors seek new opportunities in industry; we suspect that the typical reason for such a move is to improve one's salary but certainly changes in life circumstances sometimes require a change in geography. Some people move into federal government roles because of a sense of mission and attraction to the relative job security government jobs offer. Some people move into state and local jobs as well, but this is a topic we do not cover in this book because although we personally know and work with state and local government social scientists we do not have direct experience working in these roles.

Having made these points, there is a decent chance that you know professors who seem to be fixtures within a program at some given university. This is because, compared to other jobs described in this book, being a tenured professor comes with a number of protections that promote job stability. Therefore, for many professors, once they achieve tenure, they stay in the same job for the majority of their career. Or if they change universities they negotiate being awarded tenure at a new university before they accept a new offer. There does seem to be a notion

DOI: 10.4324/9780367815974-7

"I CAN BITE PEOPLE. I HAVE TENURE."

Cartoon 7.1

Source: CartoonStock

that earning tenure means having a job for life. We have certainly heard this at different points in our own careers. And tenure is certainly seen as an award. However, in terms of the "job for life" idea, this is not true. Tenured professors can lose their positions for reasons other than engaging in terrible personal behavior. Programs sometimes experience financial exigency (meaning they are not financially viable) and so can close,[1] and in these cases universities might or might not be obligated to find new roles for faculty. And tenure can be seen as an award but it also represents a responsibility. Tenure means, among other things, a responsibility to pursue research findings, share them in their teaching, and fairly evaluate students. Tenure is designed to protect academic freedom so that professors can explore topics through their research, sometimes controversial ones, without fear of job loss. The idea of tenure should also help ensure that faculty have a voice when it comes to university decisions and, ideally, push as needed for academic values.

Despite these clarifications about the seeming stability of being a tenured professor, it is still the case that this role is considered by many to be stable because it implies having an indefinite academic appointment; problems have to be quite serious before job loss is a serious threat. Furthermore, another benefit of tenure is it comes with academic freedom, so professors can pursue research and projects with some personal agency. This makes holding a tenured job in academia attractive to many, and it can be difficult to obtain these positions. They are quite competitive, and one normally has to undergo an extensive job search process when trying to become a professor. Cover letters, an academic curriculum vitae, statements of teaching philosophy, sample writings, reference letters, and publications can alone lead to hundreds of pages worth of application documents. Most interviews start with phone screens, then extensive two- to three-day campus visits and "job talks" (where one provides an overview of a research agenda) and sometimes it is necessary to prepare and present a lecture. Given the rigors usually tied to securing a job in academia, and tenure, one does not give it up easily. But this is not unheard of and we can demonstrate why this is true by describing a person who is loosely based on a couple of people we know. We'll call this person "Jonah."

Jonah's background: Jonah was originally pre-med but then took sociology courses in college and never looked back. After a period of working in the "real world," he realized he could pursue his interests in health and culture by pursuing a Ph.D. in sociology.

Now, Jonah has been tenured at two different state universities but gave up the role and currently works for a corporation. Importantly, he also gained applied and corporate experience before becoming an academic. Hence, Jonah can move between these worlds and has some insights into "going back to academia," whether this means returning to a higher education setting for the first time after completing a doctoral degree or perhaps returning to a professor role after leaving it.

7.1 "JONAH'S" CAREER PATH STORY

Jonah experienced an early career path that many academically minded readers will share, and that is he had a desire to step into a professorial role right after completing a doctoral degree, but found slim pickings. This was a distressing time for Jonah even though with the benefit of hindsight and experience, he worried too much. Many readers will appreciate the sense of anxiety around obtaining that first post-Ph.D. job. Jonah graduated from a fine doctoral program with well-connected professors who wrote strong letters of recommendation on his behalf. He presented at major conferences about a half-dozen times and even published a peer-reviewed journal article, albeit in a very small and highly specialized journal. Jonah completed a course on how to teach, during which time he taught a course to undergraduates and despite some learning curves walked away with decent course evaluations and a fairly sharp teaching statement. Jonah also developed experience working as an analyst on grants professors pulled in and was even the advisor for a master's program. All in all, Jonah was in pretty good shape. Nevertheless, he had a tough time finding a professor job because there just weren't many opportunities.

Life is however strange, and Jonah did make it to the phone interview stage for an Ivy League university. Every now and then, one hits an unexpected home run (or if you like, is lucky when scoring a goal in football). Despite his preparation, he was nervous during that call and whether his nervousness mattered or not, Jonah did not make it to a campus interview. But in retrospect this experience gave him some confidence that his cover letters and academic CV had at least some merits. As the year went on, Jonah found he was in contention for three visiting professorships. These are non-tenure-track temporary jobs and the primary message is: don't plan on buying a house if you take one of these gigs. A visiting professorship can provide an opportunity to gain some experience and build a profile, and department chairs might sometimes sell the point that there is a chance that one will be competitive if there is a tenure-line job that opens up during your, well, visit. But again, do not plan to stay. In Jonah's case, he was interested in starting a family and would have taken one of these jobs for the experience but they were not very appealing. Hence, some anxiety started to set in as the academic year came to a close as Jonah marched on toward defending his dissertation.

A big break came when Jonah learned about consulting firms and their interest in hiring social science Ph.D.s. Jonah learned that there are a few dozen of these firms and they offer excellent opportunities. And though one might be on "soft money," meaning salary is dependent on winning a portfolio of projects that can support staff, it is also true that these firms employ staff who are very good at winning work. Jonah learned about these positions through on-line searches and attending professional conferences. Interestingly, he did not learn much about these jobs from the faculty in his department, probably because these faculty lived the life of professors. They knew academia quite well, but their understanding of consulting was limited. Whereas they knew a lot about applied professional jobs in their special arenas (e.g., school psychology professors know a lot about applied school psychologists), most of their experience with applied research work was rooted in winning the occasional grant designed for faculty. Furthermore, Jonah did not express any interest in consulting firms when in the classroom because he did not know enough to ask about jobs with such companies. As a result, Jonah co-constructed a reality with his professors wherein the focus was on securing work in academia, and Jonah was not advised otherwise. So for a few months, he dutifully applied for the few assistant professor or visiting professor positions that showed up in job boards, wondered what it might be like to live in Georgia, Idaho, or wherever, and hoped for the call that rarely came. When he did receive a call, Jonah performed a lot of research to understand the institution by reading and re-reading the job description, poring over website details, thinking if he knew someone who was somehow connected to the university who might give me some insight, and working out how he might be a really good fit for a job. But the cold hard truth was that he was competing in a very large pool of applicants; he was up against at the very least dozens of other well-qualified candidates. In the end, Jonah pulled out of academic job searches because he learned more and more about consulting.

His big breakthrough came at a professional conference that offered a robust job search system. It doesn't matter which one, if the conference is large and sponsored by a large group (e.g., it starts with a word like "National" or "American" or "European") it will likely have a robust job-matching system. This conference, in the particular year Jonah was growing desperate to find a good post-Ph.D. job, was held in Chicago, IL, in the United States. He expressed interest in about seven different positions, received seven on-site interviews, and he was competitive for each role. The whole experience was different. Jonah went from applying for a job by mailing in an application (back then we all still used snail mail) and expecting to hear nothing for weeks and months, if he were to hear anything at all, to interacting with recruiters who followed up promptly with information about what they were looking for and next steps. During this process, Jonah drew on his experience from outside of academia. Prior to graduate school, he worked in social service and corporate settings for five years. He was even a human resources recruiter for a large company, which helped but was in no way critical to a successful search process. Common sense mattered greatly; Jonah took the time to research companies before he interacted with a recruiter and thought through how his skill set might be of use to them. And

Jonah thought through how his dissertation research might connect to a company's interests. Some readers might at this point feel a little uncomfortable because their research topic is far afield from what a consulting firm might be interested in. Be flexible here. Jonah's dissertation topic dealt with understanding how mental health constructs are influenced by culture and how this idea manifested among adolescents in a country outside of his home nation, The U.S. Jonah did not expect employers to be overtly interested in that topic but he did develop skills in surveying, statistical procedures like factor analysis, Item Response Theory, ethnography, and mixed methods.

Importantly, Jonah knew how to interview people, use interview data to inform survey writing, and so on. Equally as important, by then he was accustomed to explaining his ideas and why they mattered. Employers need to know they are hiring someone who can think through abstract ideas and communicate them clearly. In job interviews Jonah spent most of his time discussing how his skill sets could help a company.

Now consider a doctoral student wrapping up a dissertation that is similarly abstract (many if not most dissertations are). Suppose the student is focusing on phenomenological approaches to understanding how college students experience artwork in textbooks. Presumably, the student pursues this line of work out of interest in how people learn. Pretend now that the student is in an interview: our fictitious student can describe a deep grasp of learning theories and the wherewithal to transform this into a research question that, if answered, contributes to the knowledge base. Add in the capacity to clearly communicate ideas and willingness to learn more can go a long way toward impressing prospective employers.

Getting back to Jonah, he landed a job with a widely known firm that is based primarily in Washington, DC. Jonah moved there and found himself in a two-bedroom apartment roughly one week after he defended his dissertation. A week after that he was on the job and billing time and in a month he received his first pay check, which was noticeably larger than what a visiting professor typically makes, and it came sooner because Jonah worked during the summer! And at this point Jonah realized that he wanted to have a comfortable lifestyle. He was ready to support a family and even engage in some charitable giving. Having thought about this for a long time, Jonah understood that he does not care about money for its own sake; he does however care about the relative freedom and security it brings. Jonah does not need a large salary, but he did want more than what visiting professors typically earn, given his priorities. He still cares greatly about his research and what he can contribute to his field. An important point, to which we (the authors) will return to later in this section, is that some of our academic colleagues seem to have assumed there is a choice here: earn better pay or work on what you want to work on. Indeed, we have seen some variants of this diagram bandied about academic departments over the years:

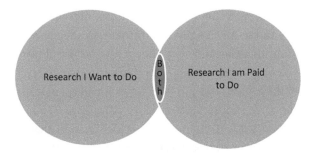

Figure 7.1 The Rare Times One Finds Research One Really Wants to Do and Is Paid to Do It

But it is possible to find ways to work on research you care about, and for respectable pay.

So there you have it. Jonah had a good start in consulting research, and he was more satisfied with his compensation and overall life situation, as compared to a visiting professor role. Many of his colleagues started the same year he did, and they never left consulting.

But one thing made Jonah different. He still thought about becoming a faculty member. Why? In part, he really likes teaching. He can hit a state of "flow" during a lecture, and even when preparing for one. He offered the occasional Saturday course in education leadership and hanging out with students who were current or future principals (or superintendents) and it would be a 12-hour day when considering early phone calls, lectures, students who wanted to chat during multiple breaks, and listening carefully as students presented to each other and engaged in group work. After 12 hours Jonah was exhausted, but it was that happy kind of tired one feels after doing something that was fun. Put another way, Jonah looked forward to even a 12-hour Saturday because he loves teaching about topics he finds to be interesting. As an aside, success begets success. Jonah received enviable teaching evaluations probably in part because of his natural excitement and colleagues who observed him offered plenty of compliments along with their constructive criticism, and Jonah listened to such feedback because he wanted to be good at leading courses. On this basis Jonah didn't want to give up on the chances of entering academia despite landing a consulting gig. More broadly, Jonah likes college campuses and the general vibe of universities. For all of these reasons, he knew that he would like to be a professor.

Putting aside the fact that there are comparatively few attractive positions in academia as compared to consulting, and there were two barriers for Jonah to address: (1) the publish or perish concern and (2) the need to get grant dollars. Taking on the latter concern, as it turns out, was surprisingly easy. In consulting work the lifeblood of any consulting organization is external grants and contracts. This is simple; consider that a law firm without clients is no law firm and a hospital with no patients is no hospital. In the same vein, a consulting firm with no grants or contracts is just a bunch of unemployed Ph.D.s. To survive in consulting, you absolutely must be able to contribute to securing grants and contracts, which is a topic covered elsewhere in this book. Jonah stayed in consulting for five years and by necessity learned to be pretty good at the proposal writing and business development process. Through his consulting work, Jonah had hands-on experience with learning about different funding sources, priorities of large clients that also happen to fund a lot of university-based work, and he developed some grant writing techniques that he still uses to this day; skills he did not learn as a graduate student. Jonah of course learned several important prerequisite skills and this is not to be underestimated, but in five years' time he developed more on-the-job grant pursuit experiences than many seasoned professors. And Jonah could tell this was the case because he kept tabs on colleagues who went the visiting professor route and stayed in touch with professors from his department, and in day-to-day conversation it was plain that their daily work was not focused on grant pursuits. So, Jonah remained interested in perhaps becoming a professor and he had developed a track record of winning external dollars. So check that box.

This leaves the publish or perish concern. Jonah knew full well that professors who do not publish often are typically not going to be awarded tenure, and it is also true that a publication record is needed to pursue the more desirable tenure-track jobs in academia. Now, there is a lot of variation around publication expectations for professors. Some teaching-oriented positions do not expect much in this regard and some programs that tout themselves as top-rated ones in high-research activity universities can have really high expectations in terms of both volume and prestige of outlets (i.e., one has to publish often in top-rated journals within a given field so that one is positioned to be a nationally recognized expert if working in a high-research activity university). In between are professorial positions that come with moderate publication requirements (i.e., universities that do not expect faculty to carry out high levels of research activity). Therefore, except for teaching-oriented roles, the publish or perish phrase applies, and even in teaching-oriented roles it's a good idea to publish once in a while. In short, if one wishes to be a professor in a U.S.-based university, publish a few pieces in peer-reviewed journals. This is true even if you wish to take on a job with a high teaching load and relatively low research expectations. This is a simple point: respectable publications are good for faculty careers.

The way Jonah handled this concern, at least initially, is he focused on publishing the results of his dissertation. This raises three brief points. The first is that Jonah worked hard to make this happen. Jonah had friends who enjoyed their weekends and evenings when he stayed home and worked on manuscripts but only after he felt sufficiently comfortable in his consulting job. The second point is Jonah asked for feedback from colleagues to help him craft his message. Dissertations are complex things, and it can be a challenge to cut them down to article form. The third point is, most of us need to persevere when negative feedback and other troubles come along. This is perhaps a point that is not discussed often enough because many people do not like to be open about difficulties they face. Somehow one's standing or prestige takes a hit if it is known that an early version of a manuscript was criticized. However, most if not all of us receive some tough feedback, and it can take a couple of days to deal with the emotional aspect of near or total rejection of a manuscript. Jonah had his trials but was lucky because he had strong, experienced colleagues who co-authored the work and journal editors offered pathways to follow so that a strong manuscript might emerge in a well-regarded journal. Jonah persevered, completed some publications, and offered contributions to his field. Here again, success begets success. A couple of people noticed Jonah's publications and asked him to work on similar tasks, which led to more publications.

Jonah decided to "go back to academia" after those five years (he was returning in the sense that he had been a graduate student) and found a different job application experience. He could tell university administrators and professors about his grant proposal experience and the kinds of funds he would pursue to support a research agenda connected to his line of scholarship. Jonah did not need to offer hypotheticals when answering questions about funding and instead pointed to what grants he pursued, what grants he knew to be available, how funding would support his work, and how he would leverage this into teaching. As a result Jonah entertained four or five tenure-line academic job offers and selected a tenure-track position at a university with supportive faculty, located in a town he found to be desirable. The department he joined was well managed and Jonah had no concerns with obtaining tenure, which he accomplished in due time.

Show some teaching skills, knowledge of grants, and how funds will support a coherent line of research and put the effort into publishing, and like Jonah, you'll have the keys needed to find a job in academia. As an aside, Jonah might have reached his goals had he taken a visiting professor route. But this chapter is more about going into academia in on-traditional ways because most doctoral-level graduate students should know the traditional routes and have easy access to professors who can answer questions about these routes.

Now imagine that Jonah ends up back in consulting after a time in academia. Imagine this because, as mentioned at the outset of this chapter, professors can and do move on to other things. Sometimes professors find they can tolerate some risk after they establish their careers, and eventually one develops a level of economic security that provides some of what tenure affords (a sense that if some endeavors do not work out, you'll still be okay). Still, why leave a tenured position? Perhaps Jonah had a chance to work on high-impact projects that can culminate in actionable information that policymakers can use and had access to a large professional staff who could make it all happen. And former professors who like their scholarship can still write and publish. To another point, former professors can, if they wish, still serve on dissertation committees, provide guest lectures, and have a mentorship role for early career scholars. Jonah might decide later in life to seek a job as a professor again. If one stays active in these ways, it is feasible to move back and forth between academia and seek jobs that are of interest without restricting professional moves within academia.

This does take some confidence, however, and such confidence might be cultivated by some of these ideas:

- Know yourself. If you love teaching, or even suspect that you do, consider being a professor. This characteristic will show through when you provide lectures, interact with students, and when you talk about the act of teaching in interviews. If you do not love teaching, find something else to do. There are plenty of pathways where you can offer important contributions and enjoy a fine career.
- Be a good communicator. Constantly think about how you can communicate your ideas in writing (and in professional presentations). Explaining the meaning and importance of your work is a major key to success, whatever your career path.
- Learn how to navigate your area(s) of interest. Learn the pathways (e.g., funding sources, publication outlets) that will allow you to fund your research ideas and describe your results. If you have a solid understanding of these pathways and demonstrated success in walking them, you should find that you can obtain jobs in academia and even move with confidence between the world of being a university professor or taking on some other Ph.D.-level job.
- Persevere. Persevere in the face of setbacks and criticism, be it constructive or otherwise. *You will almost certainly experience setbacks, and more than one. Hang in there!* Let your perseverance help when pursuing publications and grant opportunities. If you are (or become) accustomed to persevering, learn how to navigate your profession, communicate and know the intricacies of what excites you then you'll have great answers to the question: *What if I Decide I Want to Go (Back) Into Academia?*

NOTE

1 Furthermore, whole universities/colleges can and do close down.

Eight

Being one's own boss can seem romantic to many – making your own hours and implementing your own vision. But it can be challenging, and entail long hours, income fluctuations, and uncertainty. Depending on one's risk tolerance, it can be very rewarding and allow for greater work/life flexibility, though there can be a sharp learning curve as one has to take on responsibilities for jobs related to a business that one might not have had experience with previously. The economic and social disruption that occurred due to the pandemic spurred an unexpected start-up boom as people either sought to replace income lost due to job loss or in a time of existential angst decided to finally attempt to make their passion projects their main sources of income.[1] According to information collected by the Census Bureau on business formation, there was a big jump (about 85% adjusting for seasonality) in the numbers of businesses formed in the United States between May and July 2020 at the start of the pandemic, and the numbers have remained elevated since then.[2]

The mythology surrounding the tech industry makes it seem like entrepreneurs are young people developing their businesses in their dorm rooms and parents' garages; however, on average the age of most successful entrepreneurs is 45. In their much-cited study, Azoulay, Jones, Kim, and Miranda (2019) found that middle-aged founders are more likely to be successful, on average, with a 50-year-old founder being 1.8 more times likely to achieve upper-level growth than a 30-year-old founder.[3] The authors of this study argue that this is consistent with theories linking entrepreneurial success to the accumulation of human, financial, and social capital, which tends to increase with age.

Being an independent consultant is common enough among evaluation professionals that the American Evaluation Association has a section dedicated to this career path. This does not mean, however, that one should start a business right out of graduate school. From Stacey and John's personal experience as owners of different businesses, learning the way the industry works, learning how to write proposals for contracts, developing

DOI: 10.4324/9780367815974-8

experience working on projects in teams, and gaining contacts in the field helps extensively since you often get work from people you know. Prior to starting her own business, Stacey had worked at both large and small consulting firms, through which she developed extensive experience working on K-12 educational program evaluations and other aspects of educational research. Though Stacey received good (arguably elite)[4] training as a researcher in graduate school, working at these organizations gave her a excellent sense of how billing and account management works. She also got experience developing proposals and working on contracts with tight timelines, which was experience she could only get on the job. Working at these places also allowed her to develop contacts who also subsequently moved to other organizations, giving her a network of potential clients to draw on once she went out on her own.

This is not to say that everything was rainbows and unicorns even with prior job experience. When you are out on your own, there are income fluctuations and initially you do *all the work*, both the research and tasks related to business administration (recall from prior chapters all of the specialty roles a Ph.D. can adopt, focusing on contracting, proposal writing, data collection, analyses, reporting writing, etc.; now imagine needing to be good at these tasks by yourself). Capabilities for proposals are based on your qualifications, until you find more team members. It can also be isolating with a lack of easy access to others to discuss ideas.

This chapter assumes that you will be setting up a business providing services related to having a degree in the social sciences, like Stacey did, though some of the tips could be useful for people switching careers. Also, though some of the tips might be useful for starting a business outside of the social sciences because there are certain commonalities in all businesses, general business start-up advice is not within the focus of this book. Some important questions to consider before starting out are:

1) What services are you going to provide?
2) Who will be your clients?
3) How will you market yourself?
4) How should you structure your business?
5) What are the interim and end goals?

In this chapter, we address these questions and others. Again, one should consider one's own personal situation when considering opening a business. If you can answer these questions for yourself, you will be on your way to having the fundamentals of a business plan. You also do not have to answer these questions in the order presented since the answers to some of them are interrelated.

8.1   WHAT SERVICES ARE YOU GOING TO PROVIDE?

One of the first steps in creating a business is to think about what product or services you will provide. Do you want to be a technical assistance provider (i.e., teaching people how to do something)? Do you want to do primarily quantitative data collection and analytics for others? Do you want to conduct qualitative data collection and analysis? Both? Do you want to be a full-service research firm doing everything from research design to report writing? Or you want to focus on technical writing? Do you want to have a database and sell insights to others, which would be more of a product focus versus service focus?

The services or products you provide relate to your vision for your company and what problems you are trying to solve. Clients have pressure points that you can help address through your product and services. Getting a thorough understanding of your potential clients' needs will help with developing products and services. Some of this is iterative and constantly evolving since you learn more about your clients as you work with them.

Some of the services you can provide might also depend on changing trends and new technology. When Stacey was in graduate school doing data analyses using a mainframe computer running Unix, data analysis was an obscure field since one needed access to expensive statistical software and computing power was a scarce resource. There were some analyses then that would need to be run overnight, that common statistical software can now run in seconds. The biggest datasets were collected at the federal level since the government was the only entity with the resources to do so. Now innovations in data collection are happening in private industry and data are everywhere.

Data are also, collectively, a product in and of itself. This includes not just the data collected through our electronic interactions, but surveys conducted in order to sell insights from the results. Insights from data can also be a product. Though one can conduct analyses as a service, insights and predictions can be a product. Probably the most well known in the current environment are predictions regarding the spread of and mortality rates related to COVID-19. Johns Hopkins University became an early trusted resource for data, though some news outlets such as the *New York Times* have gotten into the mix.

Though this discussion is focused on quantitative data and analysis, your business could also provide qualitative data collection and analysis services. There is still a role in research for in-depth interviews, focus groups, observations, and content analysis of documents. Some of this might come into play in terms of compliance monitoring, and is often used in program evaluations as an additional layer of data to understand any implementation challenges programs have faced. There is also a long history of using focus groups in market research.

8.2   WHO WILL BE YOUR CLIENTS?

In addition to thinking about what your product or service will be, you need to think about who your clients will be. Developing your product or service will likely go hand in hand with thinking through who your clients will be, since, as mentioned earlier, typically you want to solve a particular problem or fulfill a particular need. One fundamental question though is whether you will serve individuals or businesses.

Much of the business of consulting is focused on serving other organizations. Regulations for doing business with organizations often vary across economic sectors. Government procurement differs extensively from doing business with corporations, as does the length of the contracts, the pace of the work, and often the products required.

This is not to say that one cannot use their social science background to serve individuals. Clearly practicing psychologists do this every day. One can also use knowledge of a particular area to become a coach. There are examples of social scientists who study organizations and management becoming career coaches, and those who study education helping parents navigate various hurdles in the education system, such as getting all the services promised according to laws regulating special education.

8.3   HOW WILL YOU MARKET YOURSELF?

How you market your business will depend to a certain extent on the product or services that you are providing, as well as aspects of the environment. For example, businesses that depended on in-person marketing pre-pandemic are having to adjust in the time of COVID-19. Part of your marketing plan will be a discussion of how you distinguish yourself from the competition. Distinguishers could be the services you provide as well as the methods you use, or expertise in a specific area or segment of the economy. Client treatment can also be a distinguisher. Professional soft skills such as timeliness, consistency, and communication skills are also important.

One commonality among successful businesses, both pre- and post-pandemic, is that they have a website describing their products and services. A website is the first thing people check for when they hear about a business and is an indication that you are serious. There are low-cost options for creating a website, so cost shouldn't be too much of a barrier to creating a website. Time a barrier might be, but more on that later.

Aside from having a website, a decent amount of marketing, at least at the start, might be to people you worked with previously. This is likely part of the reason why a lot of successful entrepreneurs tend to be older – they have a network of people to call on.

Beyond the website and networking with former coworkers or others you know in the field, there are a plethora of options for marketing. Which ones are right for you and your business will depend on both your business and, to a certain extent, on your personality. In economic terms, there are also opportunity costs for all marketing activities in that they can potentially take time away from other business activities. For example, though blogging is touted, it is something that once you commit to doing it, you need to do it regularly. However, blog writing might be a better approach to marketing for someone who is a bit more introverted and/or if you are marketing to people that are more likely to read a blog than do extensive in-person networking at conferences and local networking events for business owners.

Some businesses benefit from getting various certifications, particularly for government contracting, though large corporations also have supplier diversity programs. For example, there are certifications for women-owned small businesses, businesses operating in economically disadvantaged areas, veteran-owned businesses, minority-owned small businesses, and combinations of these different designations. Having these certifications do not guarantee winning contracts but can be used as part of a larger marketing plan and advertised to potential clients. These certifications can also provide you access to networks of businesses and conferences where you can sell your services. Indeed, some federal contracts large firms pursue provide bonus points when a bid entails partnering with business with these designations so you will be an attractive partner if you can and do register your business with one or more of these designations.

In general, marketing typically includes some mixture of social media, email marketing, referrals, and in-person networking (at least pre-pandemic). You can often hire other firms to do some of this work for you. You can hire firms to help you market on LinkedIn, write blog posts, send out your email marketing, etc. Larger firms may hire public relations firms to try to get them in the news. Given that you can spend a lot of money and time on marketing, you really want to think through where you can get the most "bang for your buck."

8.4 HOW SHOULD I STRUCTURE MY BUSINESS?

As someone with a Ph.D. in sociology, Stacey had limited to no experience with business administration when she started out. She had studied work and family issues in graduate school and had been an employee at organizations of different sizes but had not actually run a business before. There was a sharp learning curve as she learned about setting up email and dealing with invoicing. She also had to give serious thought to how to structure her business since that information was required for registering the business with the state.

All business structures have pros and cons in terms of the effort it takes to set them up, the amount of liability each exposes you to, and the tax requirements. The requirements for setting up businesses and taxes and fees one might be responsible for vary by state and jurisdiction so readers should discuss their particular situations with an attorney and a tax professional. One might also want to discuss potential liability issues with an insurance professional. Errors and omissions insurance is an insurance type that is recommended for consulting and evaluation work. Some institutions are also asking consultants to demonstrate that they have cyber insurance to protect against liability from leakages of data containing potentially identifying information (PII).

In the United States, business structures tend to fall into five broad categories: (1) Sole Proprietorships, (2) Partnerships, (3) the aforementioned Limited Liability Companies (LLC), (4) For-profit corporations, and (5) Nonprofits. Legally these are not always mutually exclusive categories. For example, corporations can be LLCs and nonprofits are often established as corporations. We provide some general descriptions of each and readers should consult with legal and tax professionals to decide which organization type is right for them.

For-profit, sole proprietorships and partnerships are easy to set up and potentially less complicated from a tax perspective, though they potentially expose the owners to more liability since there is no difference between the owners and the company for liability purposes. Partnerships allow for the sharing of work burden, but there is still potential for owners to be exposed to liability.

A Limited Liability Company (LLC) is another type of for-profit business that is more complicated to set up but also protects the owners from some liability by creating a separation between the owners and the business entity. There might be more taxes involved with this business type depending on the state where it is located. For sole member LLCs (where the LLC has only one person as both owner and employee), the business entity is disregarded for tax purposes and owners can report business income as self-employment income on their tax returns. Once there is more than one person, separate tax returns will be needed for the owners and the organization.

For-profit corporations and nonprofit organizations are similar in that regulations for both require a board of directors and minutes from board meetings. For-profit corporations can be further classified as S-Corporations and C-Corporations, which have different tax implications. Nonprofits need to fulfill multiple requirements to obtain and maintain tax-exempt status from the IRS. Nonprofits can establish themselves as trusts, associations, or corporations.

Some of the decisions about how to structure your business can be informed by whether you want to have employees, contract work out, or both. Though you might be able to do all the work in your organization, do you want to? Some business owners do not want to have a lot of employees. Even so, would it make more sense to hire some of the work out? When Stacey started her own business, she contracted with professionals to design her website and marketing materials, leaving her more time to do the work she was interested in.

Paying for services is one factor among many in deciding how much you charge for your work. To paraphrase advice Stacey received: if you're not making money from what you are doing then you have a hobby, not a business. Market rates can act as a guideline for how much you charge, but you also need to consider other business and personal factors. At a basic level, your personal income or profit is what you make once your business expenses are paid. This will be the amount that will be taxed. There are certain business expenses that will be inevitable, such as insurance, equipment, business taxes, and paying for certifications and marketing. Your income will then need to pay for your personal expenses such as housing, food, clothing, taxes, insurance, and childcare.

In addition to fixed personal expenses, there are lifestyle factors one must consider. How much vacation per year would you like to take? Sick time? How much do you want to contribute to your retirement account? How many hours per week can you realistically work? Working 80–100 hours a week might be sustainable in the short term, but it is a recipe for burnout over time. Also as discussed earlier, if you decided it makes sense to hire out various services, then those services will need to be paid for. Some of these lifestyle goals will inform what the end goal for your business is.

8.5 WHAT ARE THE INTERIM AND END GOALS?

Having a business is a lot of work so it is good to understand what you are working toward. At the beginning it might be to just break even, but eventually there will be other goals that can be used to focus your energy. This can change over time, but usually business owners develop interim goals to guide their efforts toward their ultimate goal. Is the end goal to be bought by another company? Do you want to leave the business to your children or other family members? Do you want to have creative control over your own time during your career and then close it when you retire? Having a sense of what your end goal is can help guide your decisions as you go along.

This does not mean you have to have the next 20 years planned out. Indeed, even if you have a five-year goal, you need short-term milestones as guideposts to assess whether you are on track. These goals and milestones, as well as strategies to achieve them can be laid out in a business plan, which does not have to be a long document as long as it is well thought out. Some owners review their progress toward achieving the goals in the plan annually and then adjust as needed in response to market conditions or other factors. Also, achieving one goal can often lead to another goal becoming in reach that you had not considered before, so taking a step back and assessing your goals regularly can help in building your business.[5] Having an end goal can help though when obstacles inevitably present themselves it might be time to shift gears. Sometimes you can reach the end of what is possible in a given environment and at a given level of effort.

In closing, having a business can provide you with independence and creative control, though it will come with many tasks that go beyond what you might consider as your primary occupation. There will likely be some income instability at the start which can be stressful, though on the flip side your earning potential is technically unlimited. Thoughtful planning can increase the likelihood of success.

NOTES

1 Rosalky, G. (2020, December 4). New businesses starting at record rates despite the pandemic's effect on economy. NPR. Retrieved May 18, 2022.

2 Census Bureau (n.d.). *Business and industry: Time series/trend charts*. Retrieved June 14, 2021, from www.census.gov

3 Azouley, P., Jones, B. F., Kim, J. D., & Miranda, J. (2019). *Age and high-growth entrepreneurship*. Retrieved August 3, 2020, from www.kellogg.northwestern.edu/faculty/jones-ben/htm/Age%20and%20High%20Growth%20Entrepreneurship.pdf

4 Stacey's coauthors pushed using this description.

5 Taking a step back and assessing your overall life goals in general can also help in building the life that you want!

Nine

It is possible to work in academia and in other sectors at the same time since the boundaries between these are somewhat porous. The most obvious pathway for doing so is to teach on a part-time basis. Another idea is to maintain skill sets and a work record that is needed in academia and another setting. What might be less obvious is how to maintain such a record.

One approach that works for academia, consulting, and government contracting (see Chapter 2) is to develop expertise in grant and contract proposal work. Money is the lifeblood of organizations and knowing how it is transferred across types of organizations within your area of expertise can make anyone an attractive job candidate. In Chapter 1 we described how there has been a reduction in the number of tenure-track faculty positions. However, it still appears to be the case that prospective faculty who can point to a history of securing grants will have a much easier time landing a job, and faculty who engage in research (be it pure basic research, use-inspired research, pure applied research, or some combination of the three)[1] will likely be able to describe how their work might be of interest to other types of organizations.

It is true that one has to be creative, manage time, manage it well, and still work hard to pull this off, but securing grants, doing the work, publishing findings, getting your name out there, all help to create a kind of snowball effect, or a virtuous cycle, that provides the basis for flexibility in career choice. In terms of being creative, suppose for a moment that you are working on a grant or contract for a private firm and you generate a series of proprietary findings, meaning you cannot publish the results. Or sometimes the results are to be made public but the publication, whatever it is, does not have your name on it. The work might be meaningful and complex, but typically it will not yield much currency in terms of academia. After all, one must publish or perish. We have found that even under these circumstances, being a little creative can go a long way. For example, publishing findings might

DOI: 10.4324/9780367815974-9

not be possible, but can you publish the application of your research methods in a peer-reviewed journal? Oftentimes, the answer is yes. This can be true even if you're on fairly well-tread ground. Say you pulled off a survey, or a randomized controlled trial, or applied some statistical process but cannot publish results under your name. Look around at some methodological journals. They are out there. It might be the case that the journal editors and readership are interested in your particular application of the methods and lessons learned. Note also that some methodological journals are prestigious and have high-impact factors because most peer-reviewed articles cite methodological sources to remain scholarly and because it saves a lot of space if an author can write the equivalent of: "I used X approach to Y method, and if you want to see details See Merola (2021)." What if you are convinced you cannot publish about your methodology or you tried and your manuscript was rejected? Well, revisit that imagery of snowballing and working hard to get the snowball rolling. Try alternative outlets like blogs and conference presentations. Get your name out there so people can see your expertise. Do this enough and you'll likely get a call from a research team seeking your help and then you can obtain an opportunity that will help you publish some work.

If you're a person who lives mostly in the contracting world, publishing will still help your career. Funding agencies of course look at the resumes of applicants and being able to list peer-reviewed publications certainly goes a long way toward your being taken seriously, which is utterly necessary in competitive environments.

How might this look in an academic job setting? Think about the notion of a research lab a professor runs. This lab will entail a series of projects, typically funded by grants, and administered by professors, graduate students working in what is essentially an apprentice model, and perhaps some professional staff. In this setting, the lab can almost feel like a small business because there are budgets to consider, timelines and Gantt charts, reporting requirements, salaries to consider, and workloads to manage. This notion of a lab can easily be a bit larger. Many faculty, for example, run or co-lead university-based research centers. Oftentimes, these centers entail consortia of a few faculty and professional staff, sometimes within one college or multiple colleges in a university to pursue a shared research agenda. These larger operations can have more specialty staff; people who focus on budgeting (needed for grant applications and when conducting work), specialists who track and identify requests for proposals, grant writing experts, editors, administrative assistants, and maybe operations specialists who help ensure that your working space will not be taken over by next year's incoming freshman class. These centers can also be coordinated efforts operated by people with titles like Associate Dean for Research, and at a broad university level (i.e., at a provost or president level) there are jobs with titles like Associate Provost for Research. People in these positions take on leadership roles, should focus on mentoring and supporting faculty, carry out broad university agendas, and should have no trouble transitioning to organizations outside of academia should they ever wish to do so. If people in these positions wish to stay put, they will almost certainly be working in the world outside of academia because they often represent their university to business leaders, politicians, and the media. Many of these university staff maintain their professor rank and title in their home departments and even maintain their line of research. But by virtue of their administrative jobs, they tend to be comparatively visible both within a university and in the public, and are often asked to take on tasks that fall far outside of their research agenda.

How might this look in a consulting firm and/or government contractor? There are national experts who work in these types of firms and publish often. Their work is widely cited, and they enjoy the respect of staff in federal and philanthropic agencies. In the cases of these experts, there are at least three reasons why they do not pursue academic careers: (1) they like their current circumstances, (2) they have limited if any teaching experience, and (3) some hold traditional views of academia wherein one starts out as an assistant professor, moves on to the associate professor, and then one becomes a full processor. As discussed earlier in this book, it can take a very long time to achieve the full professor rank. Typically one doesn't start entertaining the idea of seeking promotion to this level until at least 12 years after completing a Ph.D. and that assumes maintaining an ongoing record of teaching, research (and publication) and service to one's department, college/university, and the field. One does not simply just become a full professor unless circumstances are unusual. However, some institutions might afford some flexibility assuming an applicant is early enough in a career and knows how to answer the question: "what is in it for me if I hire you?" Think about Jonah from Chapter 7. If he wanted to re-enter academia, he would have some advantages. First, he was tenured at two different institutions, and he can present syllabi he created, student evaluations of his teaching, and he can invite prospective university employers to speak to his former students. Furthermore, he could be flexible. It is not, for example, unheard of for universities to higher faculty at the associate and full professor levels without tenure, with the expectation that the new hire work hard to fit into the culture (to be blunt, try out for the team) before being awarded the responsibilities and protections of tenure in, say two or three years. Is this type of move unusual? Yes. However, many university deans will be interested in supporting the profile of their institutions if they can hire faculty with strong publication records and the high likelihood of being able to secure external funds. There is an old saying: "I can put your name on Mount Rushmore." This is not literal of course! But university administrators are no different than any other professional; they want to be good at their jobs and part of that is making sure strong faculty are around to carry out a mission. It is possible to help a dean see how hiring a person who has an ever-expanding snowball might be good for all involved.

Having offered ideas for securing positions within academia or leaving academia to work elsewhere, developing a strong command of one's research might make this question somewhat unimportant. By strong command of research we don't mean just understanding it, we mean being in a position to successfully secure funds for research and being able to publish work on a fairly routine basis. We're talking about people who, in any given year, secure grants, publish an article or two, a widely read technical report, perhaps a book chapter, and present at a conference. Say further this person has some drive to teach or mentor, which is why there is some compulsion at hand for a university affiliation of some kind. If this combination describes you (or might one day), then where you work might not be all that critical a question unless your identity is tied up in having some given title (e.g., president, owner, vice president, professor, center director, principal research associate). If you are accomplishing a lot in your field, and if you want to teach and mentor, then do not worry; this issue will almost certainly take care of itself! This is because you'll be well known enough that you'll be sought out. People with less experience in your area will want to learn from you, as well as those who know more than you do. The chances to offer guest presentations at your local university, keynote addresses, and opportunities to collaborate on a paper or book will all come so long as you stick with it.

9.1 ANY MORE ADVICE ON HOW TO GET THERE?

We should offer the caveat that we do not claim to have crossed some magical threshold into being professionally well known. The three authors of this book have been around for a while and successful enough to convince a publisher to give us a book contract. We have had some successes and we can each offer some advice on how to reach a stage where your work is snowballing and it is not particularly important if working in academia or not, outside of considerations like academic freedom, compensation, and lifestyle described earlier in this book. Whatever your job title and employer, your work is well known enough that you can have chances to teach others if not a professor, and people outside of a university will be asking for your time if you are one.

You will have to work hard and persevere through adversity. Few contracts build in time for you to work on peer-reviewed publications, and if they do it is probably not enough time. If you want to play in multiple circumstances you'll be working nights and weekends. Indeed, this book was mostly written on nights and weekends. But you'll also have to be careful not to overstretch.

NOTE

1 Stokes, D. E. (1997). *Pasteur's quadrant: Basic science and technological innovation*. Brookings Institution Press.

Ten

If you take away one thing from this book, it is this – the range of non-academic careers for social scientists is wide, varied, and many in number. Unlike in academia, there isn't one career path or one ultimate goal. With some planning and persistence, you can move between non-academic sectors and roles, as well as between academic and non-academics. You do not have to work for one organization or industry forever. This flexibility allows you to make a career that works for you and your goals. This might be scary, but it is also freeing, and you have all the skills you need from graduate school to be successful!

One unifying thread among the personal stories in this book is that the authors made career decisions based on their personal values, family situations, and likes and dislikes, rather than pressure from academic mentors or societal norms. Mercedes did not like teaching and valued stability, so went into government. John moved between academia and consulting looking for the balance of adequate compensation for the work he does, so he can fulfill his retirement fantasies, and Stacey was looking for work/life balance that was not always modeled by her graduate-school mentors. This requires some soul searching and potentially hard conversations but will be worth it as you create a career that works for you.

Once you determine your values, it will be easier to determine how a potential job or organization aligns with those values. Though you might be able to change workplace cultures in some cases, you need to consider realistically how much frustration you can handle. Indeed, this book is being completed during a period called the "Great Resignation" when workers across the economy are making their frustrations known by changing jobs.

One fun approach to thinking about these issues is presented in Figure 10.1. This should not be interpreted as a comprehensive life decision tree (it does not account for those who want to go into clinical job settings) but rather a suggested way to approach these decisions that incorporates some of what we covered in the earlier chapters.

DOI: 10.4324/9780367815974-10

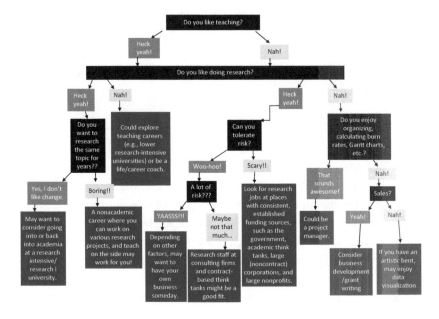

Figure 10.1 Non-academic Careers Decision Tree

By reading this book you have taken a great first step in gathering information to plan your next career step. Our goal was to give you an overview of what was possible, so you have some foundational knowledge from which to start your journey. If what you read here intrigues you, dig a little deeper and reach out to people in the areas you are interested in to get additional information.

Good luck and go get 'em! Persevere and you'll do well.

Note: Page numbers in *italics* indicate a figure and page numbers in **bold** indicate a table on the corresponding page.

academic careers: adjunctification and 3; career pathways in 80–82; characteristics of 14; demands of 4; grants and 85, 98; part-time teaching and 9, 98; publication record in 3, 85–86, 98–99; research and 98–101; returning to 78–80, 84–88, 100–101; social sciences and 6, 8–9, 20; tenure-track positions in 3–4, 78–80, 85–86

academic think tanks 29

advocacy think tanks 29

American Association for the Advancement of Science (AAAS) 76

American Association of Retired Persons (AARP) 17

American Association of University Professors (AAUP) 3

American Educational Research Association (AERA) 17

American Enterprise Institute (AEI) 15

American Evaluation Association (AEA) 22, 89

American Federation of Teachers (AFT) 3

American Psychological Association (APA) 17

American Sociological Association (ASA) 17, 30

Azouley, P. 89

big data 50

Brookings Institution 15

business structures 94–95

C-Corporations 95

communication 34–36

consulting firms: acclimation process and 21–22; career pathways in 26, 81–84; characteristics of 16, 25; grants and contracts in 33, 85; leadership in 27; limited liability companies and 8; rainmaking in 27–28; research and 100; social scientists and **15**, 16

contract negotiation 40

contract research 29

Council on Foundations 17

COVID-19 pandemic 1–3, 16, 73, 91

data collection 31–32, 37, 91–92

data-driven decision-making 2, 25

data management and cleaning **43**

data visualization 32, 39, **44–45**

entrepreneurship 89

Equitable Evaluation Initiative 17

evaluation 22–23; *see also* program evaluation

Evaluation Without Borders initiative 18

explaining and presenting **47**

external evaluation 22–23

Facebook 16

Federal Acquisition Regulation (FAR) 40

fellowship programs 76–77

Floyd, George 2

for-profit corporations 94–95

foundations 17
Foundations for Evidence-Based
    Policymaking Act (Evidence Act)
    of 2019 2

general private industry **15**, 16, 29–30
Global Go To Think Tank Index 15
Google 16
Google Scholar 52
government agencies: characteristics of
    58; grants and 58; research and 100;
    social scientists and 14, **15**, 57–58, 76;
    typical tasks 25
government contractors 14–15, **15**, 77
government hiring process: assessment
    questions 68–71; certification process
    59, 62, 71–72; federal resume/CV
    59–61; fellowship programs and
    76–77; GS pay scale 61–62;
    "How to Apply" guidance 68, 69; HR
    contacts 71; informational interviews
    62–63; interview process 72–74; job
    announcement postings 64, 64, 65,
    65, 66; onboarding process 75–76;
    position duties 66, 66; qualification
    information 66–67, 67, 68, 68;
    resume/CV review 72; selection
    process 74–75
grants and contract proposals: academia
    and 85, 98; consulting firms and
    33, 85; expertise in 98; government
    agencies and 58; nonprofit
    organizations and 17, 30

HHS Emerging Leaders Program 76
h-index 52
Hitchcock, John 10, **12**
human resources (HR) 51, 59, 68, 71

independent consultants: business
    formation as 89–91; business
    structures and 94–96; certifications
    and 93–94; clients and 92; data
    collection and 91–92; interim and end

goals of 96, 97n5; marketing 92–93;
    services provided 91–92
informational interviews 62–63
internal evaluation 22–23, 30
interviews 52–54, 72–74

job searches: benefits packages and
    54–55; data analytics and 50; Google
    Scholar and 52; government agencies
    59–77; informational interviews
    62–63; interviews 52–54; job talk
    53–54; methodological skills 49;
    OrcIDs and 52; personal branding 51;
    professional development and 49–50;
    questions to ask 54–56; resume
    tailoring and 51, 59–61; social media
    and 50–51
job talk 53–54
Jones, B. F. 89

Kelly Government Solutions 77
Kim, J. D. 89

limited liability company (LLC) 8, 12n1,
    94–95
LinkedIn 50–51

Match.com 16
McGann, James 16, 29
Meals on Wheels 18
Merola, Stacey S. 10, **11**
methodological skills 49, 99
Miranda, J. 89

National Center for Charitable Statistics 17
National Center for Educational Statistics
    (NCES) 25
National Education Association (NEA) 17
National Institutes of Health (NIH)
    58–59
non-academic careers: consulting
    firms 16, 25–28; decision tree
    104; general private industry 16,
    29–30; government agencies 14,

25, 57–58; government contractors 14–15; methodological skills and 49, 99; nonprofit and philanthropic organizations 17–18, 29–30; part-time teaching and 98; program evaluation 22–25; project management 28–29; research skills and 98–101; skills for 31–33, 49–50; social scientists and 9–10, 14–22, 103–104; think tanks 15–16, 29; types of **15**, 19–22, 39–40

nonprofit and philanthropic organizations: business structures and 94–95; career pathways in 29–30; characteristics of 17; grants and 17, 30; internal research and 30; social scientists and **15**, 17–18; tax-exempt status and 95

Obama, Barack 2
OrcIDs 52

partnerships 94–95
personal branding 51
Presidential Management Fellow (PMF) Program 76
professional development 49–50
program evaluation 22–25
project management 28–29, 36, **42**

qualitative data 32, **42**, 50
quantitative data 31–32, 50, 91–92

randomized controlled trials (RCTs) 31, 37
remote work 1–2
report writing 36, **46**
requests for proposals (RFPs) 33, **41**
research: academic careers and 98–101; conducting 84, 84; consulting firms and 100; contract 29; defined 22; external 22–23; government agencies and 100; internal 22–23, 30; non-academic careers and 98–101; project management and 28–29;

qualitative 32, 50; quantitative 31–32, 50; theory-based 32; typical tasks 23–25
research design **43**
research methods: peer-reviewed journals and 99, 102; skills for 40, **41–47**, 48
research proposals 33–36, 40, **41**
research translation **47**
Robert Wood Johnson Health Policy Fellows program 76–77
Rubio, Mercedes 10, **12**

Science and Technology Policy Fellowship (STPF) 76
scope creep 28
S-Corporations 95
skills: communication 34–36; contract negotiation and 40; cultivating patience 38; data management and cleaning **43**; data visualization and 39, **44–45**; explaining and presenting **47**; good thinking and 36–38; historically important 33–35; leadership and 36–37; methodological 49; non-academic careers and 31–33; project management and **42**; proposal writing and **41**; qualitative research and **42**; report writing **46**; requests for proposals (RFPs) and **41**; research design and **43**; research methods and 40, **41–47**, 48; research proposals and 33–35, 40; research translation **47**; statistical analyses **44**; statistical interpretation and **44**
social media 50–51
social sciences: academic careers in 6, 8–9, 20; demographic trends in 5, **5**, 6; disciplines in 5, **5**, 13n13; employment trends in 6, **7**, 8, 13n15; non-academic careers and 9–10, 14–15, **15**, 16–22, 103–104
sole proprietorships 94–95
statistical analyses **44**
statistical interpretation **44**

Teach for America 18
teams 36
think tanks 15, **15**, 16, 19n5, 29
Think Tanks and Civil Societies Program 16
Tinder 16, 19n8

Urban Institute 17
USAJobs.gov 59, 64, 76

U.S. Department of Health
    and Human Services
    (HHS) 76
U.S. Office of Personnel Management
    (OPM) 76

Washington Evaluators 18
wicked problems 2